How the Camp Fire Girls
Won World War II...

AND OTHER MEMORIES

REBECCA G. MORRIS

First edition, 2017

These feature articles and stories originally appeared in the following publications: *The New Yorker* ("The Good Humor Man," June 17, 1967; the story was made into an MGM feature film, "One Is a Lonely Number," in 1972); *The Saturday Evening Post* ("The Bellevue Circus," March 9, 1968); *New York Sunday News* ("Around the Town in 26 Hours and 36 Minutes," March 31, 1974; "The Education of a Hopeless Cook," March 21, 1976; "The Scuba Cops," June 5, 1977); *American Short Fiction* No. 3 ("Wapakoneta," Fall 1991). "The Bellevue Circus" article © SEPS licensed by Curtis Licensing, Indianapolis, IN. All rights reserved.

Cover: *Three girls at poolside* (2017). Giacomo Piussi.

For information about the book, contact campfiregirlsww2@gmail.com

ISBN 978-0-578-19387-8

Library of Congress Control Number: 2017915677

The author wishes to thank Beverly Bell, Barbara Dunlap, Giacomo Piussi, and Anne Thompson for their help in preparing this book.

CONTENTS

You've Got to Begin Somewhere 5

Growing Up at the Movies 9

Ohio vs. the World 13

Darling, I Am Growing Old 15

Wo-He-Lo 17

Prevaricator 23

Balderdash 28

The Bellevue Circus 39

The Good Humor Man 76

Wapakoneta 91

The War With New Jersey 147

Rotting Saints and Virgin Martyrs 167

Ex Votos in Naples 175

Getting to Priene 186

Around the Town in 26 Hours and 36 Minutes 196

The Education of a Hopeless Cook 208

The Scuba Cops 214

How I Became Solvent 227

YOU'VE GOT TO
BEGIN SOMEWHERE

. . . AND I SHALL. At 7:12 on this hot summer morning, I will turn eighty-five. Outside, the air is already scorching. The city is in cesspool mode again. "It's not the heat, it's the humidity," as New Yorkers say. I was born in mid-July, during an Ohio heat wave; wet, bloody, and complaining. I told them a thing or two about heat.

No one is around this blistering July day to hear me, let alone see me. I look out my window at the vapor-choked sky while sweat trickles down my cheek until I can taste it. The salt is reassuring. Lately, I've begun to feel that I'm disappearing. The face that I knew for so long has changed. I used to be taller, I think. People do disappear. Die is a euphemism. They disappear. For a while there are reminders: the monument in the cemetery where no one ever comes. My parents, those two urns sealed in a cement wall in a retirement state. Not gone entirely. I remember them still – they live accusingly in my head. Memories persist for a time – family, friends – but none are so sharp now. There are photographs somewhere in an album that no one will want. I'm the last of my line and I stuffed my forbears into a trunk – stiff portraits of strangers that my mother knew. All those staring ancestors! What can one do with so many formal wedding photographs, so expensive in their day? I do know where some of those rigid ancestors are buried: in small Ohio cemeteries – outside the towns that rose up on the land that they settled. Family plots. Years, generations, centuries. Memorials topple, the stones are hauled away, the land is turned over. People disappear.

There's not enough time now. My fault entirely. I have been writing for a living most of my adult life, extolling subjects I often barely understood, nor especially cared about. I wrote passionately about subways, hazardous waste disposal, and banking law. Put emphatic words in important men's mouths; told other women's stories. I was highly employable. But good resumes do not receive Library of Congress numbers. And that reaches my point. Decades of writing, and I've yet to get a single LCCN. Remiss of me. That identifying number may be the only memorial some writers ever achieve.

The purpose in writing – assembling – this book, read or not, is to earn an LC number. I do not want to just disappear.

With so little time left now, I must recover the only stories I really know – the ones I've been writing for all these years, between – and often despite – "real" jobs. I have old notebooks, pages of manuscript, reams of journalism, and even some early published fiction. And then there are all the "good titles" that I never got to use. I was fixated on titles. Last week, while cleaning files and tossing old papers, I found a spiral notebook. The cover is tan, bent, and has a blue Columbia seal. Grad school in the early '60s. It is jammed with good titles, some actually written, but most never used. Pages of them. I can no longer recall what stories should have been written for many of these titles. Staring at others, I hear opening sentences, and can remember paragraphs locked in my head all these years. Some were turned into fiction. Several even got printed. Amazing. I was confident back then, and believed that I would write stories for all my stirring titles. Such terrible ambition. For years, I kept adding new titles – making quick notes and hurried synopses. Now, looking at this list, I still think a few of these titles have possibilities:

"Good Friday Walking Westward." Swiped (and changed) from John Donne – probably during Miss Nicholson's Seventeenth-Century Lit class.

"Tons of Chicken Tetrazzini." ???

"You'll Never Get Out of This World Alive." A very early effort – the steel mills in northern Ohio: worker falls into a vat of molten iron. It was printed in a small non-paying quarterly. I never worked in a steel mill.

"The Grotto." My first paid story (a regional review). Student drowns another student in her convent school's "Lourdes Grotto." Revenge fantasy. Juvenilia.

"Darling, I Am Growing Old." My father's player piano. Only some hand-written notes remain. An early effort that went nowhere. Use this to begin current work?

"Balderdash." Written, but never printed. Must be somewhere? Juvenilia?

"Serendipsomania." This was to be about drinking in Greenwich Village bars, I think.

"Dies Irae, Dies Illa." My convent boarding school again? I was eleven when I was sent there.

"A Tear Is an Intellectual Thing." Intellectual pretension more likely – and stolen from Blake. Yet it certainly resounds, and many of the best modern titles were ripped.

"Jesus Wants Me for a Sunbeam." What could I have had in mind?

"Wo-He-Lo." I was a very dedicated Camp Fire Girl.

"Irv Upstairs." I'm certain that this was published in a now-defunct miscellany, but can find no copy. Was it about a vacuum cleaner?

"Chlorine Baptisms." Notes only.

"Growing Up at the Movies." Journalism. Early feminist films. Use as opening?

"Down by the O-Hi-O." Many versions exist. Too long? Finally printed as "Wapakoneta" in a good fiction journal.

"Prevaricator." Never published. My convent boarding school again. Cloistered nuns.

"Flowers That Fester." No idea.

"The Bellevue Circus." Tuberculosis Ward. This was hard work. Finally printed in the old *Saturday Evening Post*. Did I kill the *Post*?

"A Christmas Carol 395.249." A prestigious little magazine bought this. Too grim?

"The Good Humor Man." My single score – *The New Yorker* printed this years ago. They must think I'm dead by now.

There are more titles and many more notes, but I have little time to waste. All the usual narration: of being born – place, time, and family antecedents – wasted pages. I must rely on what I have already written. So many of these stories are only fragments and, like my earliest memories, simply too brief. A captured glance, a desperate memory grab. What had it felt like inside a smaller body? One's younger self? History as stunted vision? At one time, we were all much closer to the ground. And so I will begin in Depression Ohio in the 1930s.

This brief sketch was once part of a longer article on Depression Era feminist movies.

GROWING UP
AT THE MOVIES

———

"She's got chewing gum in her hair again. Why has the child got chewing gum in her hair?" my father asked.

"She doesn't like Norma Shearer," my mother explained. "Every time Norma Shearer comes on the screen, she crawls under the seat. I can't do a thing with her."

"But it's the third time this week that she's had gum in her hair," he pointed out.

My mother looked defiant and a little guilty. "Well she doesn't like Melvyn Douglas or Joan Crawford either."

It was 1936 and I was three years old.

Other tots in Ohio took naps in the afternoon. I usually went to the movies. It was still the Depression and we had just moved to a new city where my father had found a job. My mother, a homesick young woman in a strange town, was lonely. She couldn't afford a baby-sitter, so several days each week the two of us would walk all the way downtown to save bus fare, spend the afternoon in the movies, and then meet my father after work to ride home in the car. My mother reasoned that if I got sleepy during these excursions, I could always curl up on the movie house seat and take a nap. I was rarely sleepy. So by the age of six, I had seen most of the great sophisticated and romantic comedies of the 1930s.

I would sit there in the dark on the upholstered seats of the Ohio Warner, or Paramount, or Palace theaters, small feet outstretched, little hands clutching the armrests, eyes glued to the screen where Myrna Loy and William Powell, Rosalind Russell and Fred McMurray, Claudette Colbert and Clark Gable, or Jean Arthur and Gary Cooper wisecracked their way into each other's arms. I recall little of the plots; but the faces of those duos in close-up are my earliest memories. Sometimes the combinations would change – confusing me a little – but those particular stars formed a repertory company through my childhood.

My mother loved them all, but she worshipped Leslie Howard and Norma Shearer, stars who largely made me fidget. During their love scenes I would slip off my seat and spend a little time exploring the floor until the newsreel or a cartoon came on. In addition to several romantic comedies each week, we also saw romantic musicals. My mother thought the films of Jeanette MacDonald and Nelson Eddy were beautiful. But whenever Jeanette MacDonald opened her mouth, I hit the floor. Nelson Eddy, on the other hand, I liked. He always made his entrance marching straight toward the camera, followed by troops of soldiers, or riding horseback, leading the Canadian Mounties – or striding at the camera followed by ranks of frontiersmen. They all would be singing something rousing like "Stout-hearted Men" or "Tramp, Tramp, Tramp."

However, the minute Eddy spotted MacDonald, I knew a duet

was coming and unerringly dove under the seats. After a MacDonald-Eddy movie, I would tramp, tramp, tramp along downtown Main Street, bellowing at the top of my little lungs to the great embarrassment of my mother. She would have preferred a budding Shirley Temple to a three-year-old baritone.

But mostly we frequented romantic screwball comedies. My mother was addicted to these movies. To her, they represented the ultimate in sophistication. Many of the film heroines had interesting careers. They were reporters, or writers, or editors, or else they had private incomes. Even if they were only "white collar" girls, these working women were invariably spunky. They captured the attention of attractive, interesting, and usually wealthy men. Marriage generally won out even when there were mix-ups, or amusing triangles, with the right characters always ending up in each other's arms. There were rarely any offspring to contend with and the very real Depression was seldom in evidence. No wonder my young mother preferred to spend her lonely, homesick afternoons in darkened downtown movie theaters. It was the fastest way out of 1930s Ohio.

I'm not sure how all these movies affected me because I didn't remember that I had seen them until long after I was grown. However, I am sure they must have influenced me profoundly. As every Jesuit knows, if you get a child before the age of six, it's yours forever. Like many of the '30s movie heroines, I became a writer and journalist. Yet I type badly. Did I always think that I would have a handsome male secretary, like Rosalind Russell had in "Take a Letter Darling"? But it was only years later, when television began showing old movies to fill late-night time slots, that cued by some scene or phrase, I would sit bolt upright – more startled than Proust biting into his madeleine – knowing I had seen it all before. And so, bit by bit, my childhood came back to me in black and white, amusing and peopled with stars. It is the closest thing to reincarnation.

12

OHIO VS. THE WORLD

OF COURSE, IN MY HOMETOWN we were aware of the great world – those states, cities, and countries outside Ohio. Every public library had a standing world globe and bound atlases. However, I blundered into that wider world earlier than most children.

It was an ordinary afternoon when I first discovered that far-off places had agendas of their own. I must have been four, because I had just been given my first set of paper dolls as a birthday gift. "Dolls of the World." They were not even paper (I was still too young for scissors) but were made of pre-cut felt. Sturdy ten-inch figures of stiffened cloth, large enough for a child to handle. Each came with its own national costume, designed to cling, felt on felt, to its sturdy figure. And every doll, along with its ethnic outfit, was a different colored felt! There could be no possibility for a young child to mistake which native costume belonged to which doll. I cannot recall how many dolls were in the set. Perhaps a dozen? But I do remember China, Japan, and Holland. Holland, my favorite, was a pale blue. Japan may have been tan. China was undoubtedly yellow and Africa brown. Ireland must have been green. Today this would not be PC. I do not recall exactly which colors the rest of those dolls were, but for many years I confidently expected to see all foreigners wearing typical "native" costumes.

I was playing with my dolls that hot morning, when the whole world changed. I remember sitting in the middle of our living room rug, felt dolls spread out in a circle, waiting to be costumed. And the radio was on. This scene is as clear, even now, as the pattern in that rug, or our church-shaped radio across the room. I had not been paying attention to the radio. It was too early for children's programming, but my mother often "tuned in" while she ironed. Suddenly from that wooden box boomed an interruption. A voice broke into our living room declaring that the armies of Japan had just invaded China! I looked at my small felt people in horror. My paper dolls were at war!

Not long after that brutal invasion (which some historians cite as the opening volley of World War II) most of my paper dolls were busy fighting each other. I could have lined them up – Allies vs. Axis – on our rug. I was confused by such willfulness. But even as my dolls joined alliances, formed armies, fought, or surrendered, I was fast outgrowing them.

By the time Holland was invaded (when I learned that its population did not all wear wooden shoes) I had entered grade school, used scissors skillfully, and was busy cutting out paper movie stars with lavish tabbed costumes.

As the war ramped up and raged in countries far from our living room radio, I grew taller, abandoned paper dolls, learned to stand on my head, and began piano lessons.

Old notes for this title read, "Why can't you be good like Mary Ellen?" Cousin Mary Ellen was slightly older than I. She had natural dark curls that I envied, a new chicken pox scar, and was well behaved in the presence of adults. I was considered "skinny," with sharp elbows, scabby knees, and two long braids that Ohioans call pigtails. Incautious and stubborn, I generally got caught.

DARLING, I AM GROWING OLD

THE DEPRESSION WAS STILL dragging on in Ohio when the local savings and loan where my father worked foreclosed on a popular downtown piano bar – only to find itself in possession of an enormous upright player piano. My father, seeing this unwanted behemoth, got the ambitious idea that I should have music lessons. He bought it for the cost of removal and, to my mother's dismay, the piano landed, upright, in her pristine living room like a beached whale. It would not be ignored. Once a local piano teacher was found, my fate was sealed.

I really did try to learn. But the piano was always far more talented than I – and everyone knew it. The piano could invisibly finger notes, span octaves, trill long flourishes, and some of its music rolls were even duets. People who visited us watched those ivory keys magically compress and were eager to take a turn on the bench, alternately pressing the big slanted foot pedals that pumped its operating bellows. If they peered into the cabinet above the keyboard, they might also watch pierced paper rolls revolve as familiar melodies poured forth below. Everyone loved our talented piano.

I never learned to play; there was just too little incentive. Nonetheless, my cousin and I spent hours, side by side, on the piano bench, each manning a pedal – alternately up and down – producing unbelievably good professional bar music. Those piano rolls held dozens of elaborate tunes, sentimental even for Ohio then, and I still recall the repertoire. "My Old Kentucky Home" and "I Dream of Jeannie" were most often requested. As was "Twelfth Street Rag." But "Darling" was our favorite performance.

I close my eyes now and see us there, side by side on the piano bench, each working a man-sized pedal with both feet, pumping away, laterally swaying and pressing – one forward, one back – sometimes gripping the bench for extra force or emphasis. The piano keys run up and down, effortlessly, in front of us. By the speed of our footwork we can regulate the sound. We sit there, singing loudly: Mary Ellen's curls bounce and her chicken pox scar is pink. My pigtails swing behind my back. "Darling, I am growing old – old… Silver threads among the gold." Pump, pump… "Shine upon my brow today – ay." Big finale push, "Life" – go for it – "is fading fast away… So… fast… a – way." We were eight.

I never imagined "life" could really fade away. We were so healthy – nothing but future. Our lives were secure. All we really had to do was grow…

WO-HE-LO

WHEN THE U.S. WAS FORCED, abruptly, into that distant war, I was almost ten. And very much aware of what was happening. Our radio kept us alerted daily as the country mobilized. Men and boys who never dreamed of leaving Ohio were drafted and shipped overseas. Local women took jobs, manned factories, worked in mills. Wore slacks! As the entire stunned country gathered force, armed, and prepared to fight, I joined the Camp Fire Girls.

It may have been their mysterious motto – Wo-He-Lo – that lured me, which resonates like a secret incantation but turns out merely to truncate "Work, Health, and Love." Nonetheless, Camp Fire Girls were walking posters of allegiance. We wore navy-blue skirts topped by white blouses and red triangular neck scarves. And we were ruthlessly patriotic. My group's contribution to that early war effort involved collecting scrap metal, recycling tin foil, salvaging aluminum, and reclaiming old rubber bands. Four or five of us together – canny fourth graders in laced shoes and knee socks – would attack a single neighborhood. Nothing escaped our sharp, pilfering little eyes. We became indefatigable scavengers, collecting used metal with a kamikaze dedication. Few housewives could withhold their old washing machines, dented pans, rusted tools, husband's golf clubs. Or deny us an heirloom doorstop. We carried all off triumphantly.

And when our group pledged allegiance to the flag – upright and sincere in our red, white, and blue uniforms – no one could doubt our zeal. We were that good! I can see us: combed hair and jubilant faces, sagging knee socks, but great posture. We walked proudly when we weren't sneaking around someone's trash or breaking into a backyard tool shed. What inspiration! The local newspaper printed a picture of our group beside a truckload of salvage. "Local Camp Fire Girls Win Scrap Metal Drive." There we stand, proudly saluting Old Glory in front of the public library.

Yet unseen at the pointed tip of every girl's red neck scarf was a small embroidered insignia: crossed logs with a rising flame. A blazing campfire. We looked exemplary, but in our deceitful pre-teen hearts, each Camp Fire Girl carried the secret of the tribe. We worshiped fire.

Camp Fire, in its heyday, was heavily based on American Indian lore. Girls won passage by moving up four ranks: Trail Seeker, Wood Gatherer, Fire Maker, Torch Bearer. We earned these tribal levels through acts of physical skill, crafts, service, and woodsmanship. Along with special requirements, each Camp Fire rank boasted its own Indian regalia. Trail Seekers might begin earning "honor beads," small wooden spheres of various shapes and colors – each awarded for some finished task, skill, or deed. We collected these wooden beads greedily, stringing them on leather thongs into long clacking necklaces. Moving up to Wood Gatherer, a girl could choose her "tribal" name, along with some personal Indian symbols, which she worked in a repeated design onto her new leather headband. Worn "brave" style, of course. At first, this design was stenciled onto the leather; but in progressing to Fire Maker, one's headband must be personally, and painfully, beaded – threading hundreds of miniscule colored beads into one's "Indian signature."

But even though we were serious Camp Fire Girls, it was not the ranks we lusted after so much as their impressive regalia. Aiming toward Fire Maker, a girl could begin planning her Ceremonial Gown: that magnificent long garment of heavy tan fabric, fringed in darker leather and festooned with all her honor beads and awards. Becoming a Torch Bearer (think Eagle Scout) meant finally flaunting all of one's ceremonial raiment at a Council Fire. What glory!

In summer, Council Fires were held at our local campsite: Tapawingo. Here new girls were initiated and successful candidates awarded rank. Such big Council Fires usually began at dusk beside the camp creek...

It grows dark. Nervous initiates and new Trail Seekers fidget, forming an uneven circle around the towering, unlit fire. In the growing dusk, we Wood Gatherers quickly assemble – new headbands held high – and are directed by a counselor to join the circle.

It is almost fully dark now. In the distance, I can make out some older girls crossing a field, moving toward us. Outside our widening circle, it is black. Now the new Fire Makers approach. Heads turn, wooden beads sway, as we watch these goddesses join the growing circle. A door slams from the Rec Hall and Miss Thelma, the regional Camp Fire honcho, hurries toward us, resplendent in her own ritual attire. Ample fringed bosom, feathered headdress, many strings of beads. Putting on her rimless glasses, she gives the "Camp Fire Welcome." A counselor darts forward and the central pyre suddenly flames. Bright tongues of fire leap skyward, followed by gasps of admiration. New steps in the outer dark! All turn. Our beads clack. Eight magnificent Torch Bearers file in. Each holds a lighted taper. They sing: "We come, we come to our Council Fire with measured tread and slow... to light the fire of our desire, to light the fire of Wo-He-Lo." Moving gracefully, in full ceremonial attire, one by one they add their blazing torches to the leaping flames. Behind our small bright circle, the dark forest looms.

"Burn, fire, burn," we sing. "Flicker, flicker, flame." Miss Thelma raises her hand and gives the "Fire" sign. Light reflects on her glasses. In reply, each girl drops her right fingers onto the palm of her left hand and, in unison – as if following the curve of an imaginary flame – we spiral our pointing fingers upward. The black summer sky is full of stars.

This is a big Council Fire with clans of pre-teen girls in full regalia. As each new rank is conferred, awardees stand and recite its official "Desire." When Wood Gatherers are summoned, we rise together and in unison we each resolve "to strive to grow strong like the pine tree, to be pure in my deepest desire, to be true to the truth that is in me, and to follow the law of Camp Fire." What was that law? I was never actually sure. But confronted, I would have died defending it, right there on the spot.

The night is now fully dark; black trees silhouette the high surrounding hills. Below, our fire reflects on the still, black water. Suddenly, high above us, on a far-off bluff, a flaming torch is lit! A tall figure, Indian-gowned, appears there, and calls out, echoing across the dark water: "Wo-He-Lo." Circled round that blazing pyre, young hearts brimming, eyes tearing from the wood smoke, we "Wo-He-Lo" back fervently.

I KNOW I HAD THE RIGHT STUFF to succeed as a Camp Fire Girl, and am certain that I would have – had it not been for Jo.

In Ohio, we always had a dog. When I was ten we got Jo (I was reading *Little Women*). Jo was a smart, eager-to-please wire-haired terrier. She loved me, but I think she loved my father best. Dad usually had a cold beer each night when he came home from work. He bought his beer by the case and kept it in our basement. Jo loved to run down to the cellar when he arrived and bring him a beer. It was, she figured, a social gesture. Jo was not a big dog; often she had a hard time making it up the steps carrying a full bottle in her mouth. We laughed and praised her, but could not discourage her either. If we had guests, Jo was immediately off to the cellar. She would not give up until everyone had a bottle of beer. It was a great ice breaker. My parents' friends were amused and charmed. Fine.

And then one fatal week it was my turn to host my Camp Fire group. Jo loved the Camp Fire Girls on sight. She did not tarry, did not rest, until every single pig-tailed Camp Fire Girl in our living room was holding a fresh bottle of Budweiser. Those pre-pubescent girls were totally delighted – but somehow our group leader became hysterical. I assume this may be why I never achieved the final, and coveted, top Camp Fire rank of "Torch Bearer."

WHEN MY FATHER WAS DRAFTED IN WORLD WAR II, he was just a few months short of the "military deferral" age of 38. He chose to fulfill his obligation by doing defense work. This meant that when he finished his regular bank job at four, he drove across town to one of the new 24-hour munitions plants and put in a second full shift, returning home after midnight.

With this sudden disruption of schedules – and unplanned income – my parents decided it might be a good idea to by-pass our overcrowded local junior high and to send me to a respected, but much smaller, convent boarding school. This new school – "academy" – was only a few hours away by car, but with stringent gas rationing, it might as well have been on the moon.

I attended "The Mount" for two long "war years," coming home only at Thanksgiving, Christmas, and Easter. It was, indeed, an Education.

Actually, I was eager to go. An only child, I had read all sorts of popular "girls boarding school books," serial tomes full of excitement, camaraderie, friendships, and games. However, as it turned out, the cloistered nuns at the academy had not read those books.

The following short sketch – early writing and perhaps too slight – was never published.

PREVARICATOR

WE HAD BEEN SERVED SARDINES with their heads on for lunch again. I hadn't eaten mine and was feeling empty. Instead of going outside to roller skate with the other seventh graders, I took my chapel veil and headed toward the school chapel to see if I'd dropped my rosary there after mass. We weren't supposed to leave things in the pews.

When I pushed open the chapel door, all I could see was the red glow of the sanctuary lantern burning in front of the alter. I splashed my hand in the holy water, dipped my knee, and proceeded toward the front pews. A priest said our daily masses, but one of the postulants was always server and swung the censer too hard. Our front pews were often foggy.

This morning's mass had included the Dies Irae. We had been singing a lot of memorial masses lately, and some students claimed that was how the nuns made money to keep the school going. I was thinking about the Dies Irae, which is excessively mournful, humming it to myself, when I looked down and discovered that the chapel floor was too far away. It was not an unpleasant discovery – but I certainly was several inches off the ground. Instinctively, I reached out, pressing the air to support myself as if I were treading water. Instead, I rose higher. By now I was a good two feet off the floor and beginning to list. I was not alarmed: I knew perfectly well what was happening. I'd gone to primary school with the Dominicans, a chauvinistic order, who taught us the lives of their saints. Catherine of Siena, Thomas Aquinas, Peter Martyr, and of course, Saint Dominic, himself. Few of them, we were told, kept their feet on the ground. Dominican saints levitated with a frequency that annoyed the other orders.

I moved my hands slowly back and forth, pressing down, and rose gently higher. The incense was making my eyes sting. I hung in the dark above the wooden pews, wondering what to do next. In the paintings of St. Catherine, she always lifted in a kneeling position. I tried bending my legs up and tilted sharply forward, almost somersaulting. My uniform pleats flopped about my shoulders. I flailed my arms rapidly, trying to right myself again, and began floating over the dark pews toward the communion rail. I could see the gold tabernacle approach. I quickly braked, leaning back and pushing the air forward with my hands. I was beginning to get the hang of it. If I raised my hands above my shoulders, I slowly sank. When I pressed down hard again, I rose. It was all done with the hands. Kicking threw me off my axis. I tried turning, rotating slowly, suspended above the sanctuary. Below my feet, I watched flickering candles come and go and the communion rail revolve. I tried folding my hands to pray, but soon discovered that I needed my arms for balance. In panic, I reached out, pressing the air to steady myself, and rose straight up toward the chapel dome like a large navy-blue bat. I hung there in surprise, looking down. The chapel floor was far below the toes of my school shoes now, and I wondered if my underpants could be seen from below.

There was a little light coming from some clerestory windows, and I floated over to have a look. I was so interested in what I was learning that I forgot about the time. When I heard a bell ringing far off, I was dismayed. I should have been in my classroom. I raised my arms and came down for a hard landing in the center aisle. Not stopping to genuflect, I raced toward the door.

When I reached the seventh grade classroom, lessons had begun. I tried to slip in quietly, but Sister Frances motioned for me to approach. She was a strict enforcer of the rules.

"I'm sorry I'm late, Sister," I whispered, "but I was making a visit to the Chapel." I held out my wrinkled veil as proof.

"Very commendable," she said, pinning me with a hard judgmental stare. "But prayer is not an acceptable excuse for tardiness."

"Oh, but I wasn't praying," I answered hurriedly. "I was levitating." The minute it was out, I knew better.

"Have you any idea what that word means?"

No, I told myself, say no. "Yes, Sister, flying around the chapel."

"And YOU were flying around the chapel?"

I nodded my head, shoving my crumpled chapel veil deep into my uniform pocket. For being late to class and lying about it, I forfeited afternoon recreation for a month. At roll call the next morning, in front of the whole school, I had to answer "Prevaricator" when my name was called.

For long days, I spent my afternoon detention looking out the study hall window at classmates playing on the wide lawns. Then one afternoon I spied Reverend Mother walking in the Nuns' Garden, saying her office, and decided to act. I tiptoed to the detention nun and whispered, "Lavatory." She nodded without raising her eyes from her book.

The Nuns' Garden was considered off-limits to students. I was taking a desperate chance stalking Reverend Mother as she walked there.

"Please, Reverend Mother… " I stepped forward from the shrubbery.

She was surprised, but only for a second. "Leave immediately," she ordered, snapping her breviary shut.

I met her terrifying gaze. "I have to explain something," I persisted.

"I recognize you," Reverend Mother said coldly. "You're our little liar." Her eyes were skilled despots.

"That's not true," I cried. "I'm not." I glared at Reverend Mother and pressed down hard with both hands at my sides. My feet lifted immediately, and I rose straight up, as I knew I would, stopping a few feet above her head.

Her upturned face was something to see. She looked so queer and startled that I couldn't help laughing, and I tilted above her head, uniform pleats flapping.

Reverend Mother dropped to her knees on the grass and crossed herself for protection.

I knew, then, that it was all up for me: she would be implacable about this. I dared not come down. In panic, I pressed harder, and shot high above Reverend Mother, who was now holding up her scapular cross to ward off what she didn't believe she was seeing.

I was higher than the chapel ceiling, higher than I'd ever been before. But it didn't scare me at all. I tucked my knees, leaned forward, and did a perfect somersault above Reverend Mother.

Sun whitened her upturned chin and her eyes looked deranged. The wooden cross shook. A grisly rattling sound issued from Reverend Mother's lips and she pitched forward.

I wasn't sure if that sound was anger, but I continued rising to put distance between us. I was level with the second floor dorm now. I rose higher, until the red brick building dropped below my feet and Reverend Mother was a black cloth spread on the lawn. There was no going back.

I looked down on the school roof and circled the chapel dome as a farewell gesture. Then I leaned forward. My navy-blue uniform billowed out like a wind-sock as the air caught it. Above my head, the sky was an endless, untroubled blue. I smiled and just kept going.

I did not fly away. The war ended, and while life for far too many would never be the same again, it resumed. In Ohio, we got on with our sturdy pursuits, aware that we were now part of a larger – and more dangerous – world.

I finished junior high school at the academy and, with the war finally over, was allowed to return home. I enrolled in our local high school, where I eventually made friends and was, I think, happy.

BALDERDASH

IT WAS THE TERRIBLY HOT OHIO SUMMER when Joanne Bryan and I were fourteen that we finally wrote the story of Balderdash. I remember we spent most of that summer on the Bryans' porch swing, sweeping in lazy arcs over the porch rug, pumping our bare feet on the rough cocoa matting, while we sucked lemon balls and talked. It was simply too hot to do anything. Our bikes lay discarded all day, making brown marks on the grass that set Mr. Bryan muttering to himself as he watered the lawn. All afternoon we would travel back and forth on our green slatted pendulum, shaded by the clematis vines, drinking sweet icy Kool-Aid while the summer slipped away.

Out on the driveway, Jody's little sister, Cinthy, was learning to roller skate. We could hear the burning scrape, scraaaape of her skates, punctuated by cries of pain and the screen door banging whenever she drew blood. She was almost entirely covered with Mercurochrome, and we might have felt sorry for her if she hadn't been seven years old and scabby. We had promised that if she skated up and down the driveway exactly one hundred times, it would be a mile and we would give her a silver dollar. But while she believed us, she always fell down before she reached twenty and had to start all over again. That was all right because neither of us had a silver dollar. Occasionally, we did let her have one of our sour balls. We had an enormous jar of them. All lemon. Mrs. Bryan had won them at a bridge game. If you held a lemon sour ball up to the light, it shown hotly like a clear miniature sun, and when you looked away, purple spots danced on the porch walls.

I spent most of my time at the Bryans' that summer. Their house fascinated me. I was an only child and there were four Bryan children. Jimmy went to Ohio State, and Mike would be going in the fall. They seldom felt the need to speak to us, but whenever they went in or out of the house, they dipped into our sour balls, making Jody scream, "Mother, your thieving sons are back," while I made faces. Or else Mike would tell us that Joey Petruska was on his way up the street to give us a kiss. Joey was a twenty-year-old who wandered happily around the playground clapping his hands. His mouth lolled open and his head was shaped like a jelly bean. This insult stung us far more than Mike could have hoped, because we secretly feared that no one would ever kiss us – not that we would have let anyone, of course, but still we were afraid that no one would want to. We were fourteen, graceless, and flat-chested. Our knees were scarred. Jody had freckles and I still wore laced shoes. Truthfully, we were flattered by the smallest attention from Mike and Jimmy, but we were a terrible embarrassment to them. They would bring their friends in by the side door when we were on the porch.

We became authors quite by accident through the largesse of City Hall, where Mr. Bryan worked. One day he came home carrying a worn-out office typewriter that had been replaced by a newer model. We were never sure how old that typewriter was, but it was so ancient that no one else wanted it. Once we had a typewriter, we had no choice but to become writers. Mr. Bryan even supplied the paper from stocks of obsolete City Hall letterhead. Our works were dashed off and consigned to posterity beneath the names of public officials who either were dead or had not been re-elected.

Considering that we first had to teach ourselves the keyboard, our output was impressive. We immediately began to write novels. There were apprentice pieces like "The Murders in Home Room 202," a revenge roman à clef in which we managed to cast most of our teachers as cadavers. And then a more ambitious work, "Fallen Flesh," a historical saga set in ancient Rome (we hadn't taken first year Latin for nothing) and strongly reminiscent of "The Last Days of Pompeii." It was years before we were allowed to forget that one after Jimmie got a look at it. He and Mike thought our description of a bacchanalia was priceless. They would loll degenerately on the wicker porch chairs, simpering to each other, "Oh Marcellus, let's do imbibe another amphora of wine."

"Peel me a grape, Tullius."

While Mrs. Bryan was encouraging our genius with Kool-Aid, her sons informed the neighborhood, loudly, that our prose was for the "vomitorium."

When we weren't pounding away on that typewriter, it reposed, looking professional, on a card table against the porch wall. We seldom rewrote and never thought of publication. We simply took turns, one spontaneously continuing the narrative where the other left off. Events were always a surprise.

Often our friend Mary Anne Crain, "Inkie," would appear on her bike and write a few pages. Then, if Mrs. Bryan happened to be away, we'd make fudge in the kitchen to feed our muse. We made quantities of fudge and quarts of sugary Kool-Aid that summer.

If our prose was casual, our fudge was another matter. We labored over that fudge, dripping chocolate rivulets off the stirring spoon into glasses of cold water. If the drops congealed, it was supposed to mean that the fudge was ready to harden – but this was not foolproof and we produced pan after pan of chocolate syrup.

I remember chiefly the way things tasted that summer: soft grainy fudge, cold melting popsicles, sour balls, root beer. Or the way things felt under our bare feet: burning pavement, warm grass, splinters, the cold slippery soap suds on the Crains' cellar floor when we helped Inkie do the laundry, the gravel on her driveway. The Bryans' porch rug. Then finally I remember that we wrote the story of Balderdash.

Balderdash actually pre-dated that summer; it was begun as a long serial the year Jody and I entered high school. We wrote the episodes during class to keep from being bored to death. It might have remained a holograph forever if not for that typewriter.

The story took place in Managua, a city that we described as being overrun with Marines and debating teams. We got this idea from a clipping we found in the Bryans' attic. According to this document, Mrs. Bryan, then Gertrude Hayes, second affirmative, representing Painesville High School, had clinched the 1926 Ohio State debating championship for her team. Her peroration had closed with these stirring lines: "And so I say to you, 'Take the Marines out of Managua. Shall we sacrifice liberty for bathtubs?'" Jody and I were impressed.

We could never get Mrs. Bryan to tell us what the Marines were

31

doing in Nicaragua in the first place. Confronted, she wiped her hands on a dishtowel, pushed back wisps of gray hair, and smiled to herself. She was the wife of a city official, the mother of four, and she played an acceptable hand of bridge. Managua, she told us, was a period in her life that she'd just as soon forget, adding that "Anyway, it was all balderdash."

So we wrote that the Marines had landed in Nicaragua to force everyone to take baths, and we created Balderdash to be their nemesis. Balderdash was a little girl who made bathtub stoppers out of frogs. This was an odd profession for a child, I admit, but a humanitarian one because before Balderdash invented the bathtub stopper, everyone had had to use his big toe. The Managuans hesitated to bathe because of the inconvenience, which was perfectly understandable. Balderdash, with her bathtub stoppers, became the Jeanne d'Arc of Nicaragua, driving the Marines far from its shores.

She might have been content forever doing her chosen work, we explained, if one day she had not come upon a frog who was really a prince in disguise. Instead of bestowing love's first kiss upon him, breaking the terrible enchantment so that they might marry and live happily ever after, Balderdash made him into a bathtub stopper. This, as one might expect, ruined her chances. From that point, we cast Balderdash as the modest inventress of anything that came into our heads. We rewrote history to accommodate her, and transported her to the furthest reaches of the world. I can't recall what finally happened to her, but poor Balderdash suffered one horrible adventure after another that summer and one of them must have done her in.

When we got tired of typing, we sometimes cut through the dusty playground, self-consciously skirting the baseball diamond where the boys played outs and innings, and walked to the Crains'. We didn't see much of Inkie that summer. She had started to blossom into a beauty – the only real beauty in our class. None of us realized it, but the boys who played baseball had begun to appear on her porch at sundown in noisy homage to the fact.

Looking back, it seems miraculous that all our fudge, Kool-Aid, and sour balls could have blossomed into anything but cavities. Sometimes Inkie would lure us over with the description of a new box of fudge mix that her mother was supposed to have bought – one that was absolutely guaranteed to set in ten minutes. Deluded and greedy, we would arrive only to hear the washing machine pumping away in the Crains' cellar, where Inkie toiled through the family wash. We weren't uncharitable, but we often felt that we'd been taken in. Inkie's mother worked, her brother brought his work shirts home, and Nancy, her older sister, had a summer job. They left Inkie home alone with piles of laundry and admonitions.

So Jody and I would clamber down the dark steps to the basement, where the washing machine, attached to a single light-socket, groaned, churning suds back and forth and onto the cement. Inkie would look guilty, sweating in shorts and a T-shirt. Her hair curled in the steam, and she kept it off her neck, secured becomingly to the top of her head with a clothespin. The cellar reeked of damp and Super-Suds and Clorox. The three of us slid around on the soapy water, coaxing clothes to squeeze through the wringer and trail stiffly out the other side into a basket. The wringer sucked at our fingers and tried to draw our arms into the rollers along with the clothes. Or else it would become choked with sheets and produce raucous, frantic noises, making us leap out of the way in alarm while it vibrated rapidly up and down on its wheels and Inkie tried to hit the safety release with her fist.

Our toes became clean and wrinkled from spilled bleach, and when we dragged the laundry basket up the steps – one of us pushing from behind, holding the clothes in – our bare soles got pock-marked from the gravel court where the lines were strung.

Once Inkie's wash was safely on the line, we all walked back to Jody's, stopping by the dairy to buy popsicles: cherry, orange, grape, or banana. Banana was the only flavor that didn't turn one's mouth a garish color. Occasionally, we put on lipstick because Bob Yankel, who played football for our school, worked at the dairy. We all shared a shade of pink. It was called "Dither" and gave the popsicles a peculiar taste. Eventually we turned up on the Bryans' porch swing, hot and sticky, making the chains creak under the weight of three.

Other afternoons, when we could summon enough energy, we took our books back to the public library. We lived close to the local branch and had grown up in its quiet rooms. On summer days the library was hot even with its wide screenless windows open to flies. Shafts of sunlight streamed across the reading tables, suspending motes of dust. Summer seemed to make the books extremely pungent; the smell of the library was one of our summer smells. We would cross the marble lobby on bare feet, cautioned by habit to tiptoe. We headed straight for the adult reading room (as high school students we had just been issued adult cards), turning our backs on the children's room, where under the W.P.A. Mother Goose murals we had begun with Dr. Doolittle and progressed through its graded stacks. The library seemed absolutely fixed: we browsed through its shelves, while the books stood in rows, eternally waiting for us.

We felt the same way about the head librarian. She had been there for ten years. We remembered a succession of children's librarians, but the head librarian, we knew, would go on forever. She was a small, brownish woman, and as she got older, and we grew up, seemed even smaller and browner. Whenever we walked away from the checkout desk with our arms full of books and saw the head librarian watching us, we would feel uncomfortably as if we were stealing her books. Inkie and I were certain that the only thing that could make a librarian happy was to get all the books back in the library again and then not ever let anyone take them out.

The head librarian knew us too. We would file silently past her desk, circle the reading tables, and head for the 816 shelf: American Humor. We read a lot of Clarence Day and Robert Benchley that summer, and we consumed detective fiction by the detective, sticking with a single sleuth until we had exhausted his series. The head librarian tried again and again to improve our taste, encouraging us to read the classics. We did succumb to the Brontës, but mostly we took the books she recommended and brought them back unread.

After a trip to the library, our throats felt as dry and dust-covered as the books. At the Bryans' we needed a quart of Kool-Aid to revive us. We carried the pitcher of clear jewel-colored water out onto the porch, where we read our books quietly, all alone, together.

I see us there. The lawn is sunlit. The house is green and gray. The broad porch extends, in shadow, across its front. The only thing that moves is the swing, monotonously back and forth. Our heads are bent over our books, our legs sprawl. We take turns pumping. It is still except for the sound of Cinthy skating. Every so often, the chains creak as one of us laughs out loud. We are suspended there, oblivious to the hours passing as if we would always be there. We would not, but that summer we could not have guessed it.

The following winter, six weeks before Christmas, most of our class took a sales training course designed for high school students. After school in the unheated gym, we learned to make out sales slips, to compute Ohio sales tax, to wrap packages with numb fingers, and to perform other dull, useful jobs. We even became adept at ringing a cash register, remembering to leap aside before the cash drawer shot out into our stomachs. High school students were needed to staff local stores during the Christmas rush. If you were a student with at least a B average, you were allowed to take a Christmas job and could be excused from school at noon. Jody, Inkie, and I got our first jobs that winter at Woolworth's. We made seventy-five cents an hour. We had really only wanted to be excused from school at noon – Inkie and I would have done anything to that end – and working sounded like fun. Everyone was doing it.

But when our paychecks arrived, they impressed us. It was the first money we had earned from the world; money of our own, not allowances pried from parents or baby-sitting fees paid by neighbors. We were officially recognized as part of the world's economy, and the world collected taxes to prove it. After that Christmas, we saw things differently. Time was never the same again. It was suddenly valuable. Children aren't aware of wasting time. We were. Without realizing it, we acquired a sense of time, and although we had not yet grown up… we lost our freedom.

The next summer, nothing was the same. Jody went back to Woolworth's and sold candy. In the evenings, Dick Lawrence, our class president, took over the Bryans' swing. Whenever Inkie and I came over, the four of us made fudge. Our fudge, for some unknown reason, had even begun to congeal. Inkie was working every day as a stock girl in the same department store where her mother worked. She was finally, blissfully, freed of the laundry, and could take her proper place as a belle. After work, Bob Yankel brought her votive popsicles and chocolate sundaes in cardboard cartons, but he was only one of the many admirers crowding the Crains' steps. I had a job folding advertising leaflets and stuffing envelopes for a local toy manufacturer. Jody and I still wrote when we could – I was saving to buy a typewriter of my own – but we carefully plotted our stories using a book from the library that gave formulas for "winning fame and fortune" by writing magazine fiction. We computed our output like misers, desiring to earn, as the book promised, "one cent a word."

Balderdash, once our delight, was abandoned to the hollow seat under the Bryans' dining room window. There, yearbooks, photograph albums, children's letters, class pictures, and Jimmy's valedictory address ("Ohio, We Accept Your Challenge") mingled, sentimentally preserved like pieces of a jigsaw puzzle that someone might put together some day.

But what I realize most clearly about that long, hot Ohio summer we swung away so carelessly on the Bryans' porch is that we did not know it was our last. We could never, after, have written the story of Balderdash.

THERE WAS NO QUESTION. I was going to college. I had decided this at the age of fifteen after reading a book from our public library. It featured a spunky heroine who struggles to win a prestigious university scholarship. The book was an eye-opener – and a summons. If a degree was what this very "classy" heroine wanted, I decided that I, too, was going to college.

I did win a scholarship – the only one offered to girls at our high school – and to where else but a small Catholic women's college. Meanwhile the graduating boys lumbered off-stage to various universities, clutching football, basketball, and other sport stipends in their out-sized hands.

Once enrolled, I did not stay long at this new "degree granting" convent, although its nuns were not cloistered and some even boasted academic credentials. I had been there before. Academically limited, and rule-bound, it forced too many foolish restrictions on young women, who needed to become independent.

Which is how I found myself, aged nineteen, riding the bus to a local division of our State University – "working my way through college" as a lifeguard and swimming instructor.

I left Ohio in the mid-50s, clutching my hard-earned degree, and entered graduate school at Columbia University – "in New York City," as I always added for Ohioans. I met James there and the following winter we married.

It was while we were working – and still graduate students – that I became ill…

THE BELLEVUE CIRCUS

"Ah, is my car." Raquel pointed down at the brown Volkswagen in the doctors' parking lot. She spoke shyly and when she looked at us her black eyes shown. "He look like a roach."

Harriet and I screamed with laughter. It was spring, and we were leaning out of a window on the second-floor women's TB ward, smearing soot across the fronts of our bathrobes. Five of us – Raquel, Juanita, Marta, Harriet, and I (let me say here that all the names and certain identifying details in this account are fictitious) – were playing a game Juanita had invented. Our games were simple – Harriet and I knew no Spanish; the others "had English," but not much. I had already chosen a black Bentley; now Juanita Menandez pointed to a green Jaguar and claimed it.

"Ah yes," she said, satisfied. "Yes. In my car I will drive past Carlos Menandez eighty mile thee hour." She steered the air. "I blow thee horn." She pounded the air – "bwa-a, bwa-a" – and stepped on the gas. "Ooops! Too bad. Good-bye, Carlos Menandez, you are a rat!"

We all looked down on the floor where Carlos Menandez lay, squashed flat. "Rat." We wiped our feet on him.

Marta Vasquez was looking out another window, sulking. She had finally settled for a white Buick, but she wanted two cars and we had told her she could only have one.

I had come to Bellevue as a runaway from a sanatorium far upstate. I had spent a long winter there in a green-metal bed on a glassed-in porch, watching the snow fall. I had learned to knit socks, to eat liver, and to consider myself, despite my healthy appearance, an invalid. It was an artificial world, confined to one wing of the sanatorium, heavily and brightly glassed, the reverse of one of those scenic paperweights – we looked out at the shaken snow and saw that *it* was real.

The day the sanatorium doctors told me that although my TB was almost arrested, surgery was advisable, I bolted. That night I caught a late bus south. In New York, weeping, I informed my young husband that I preferred to die in the city. And against everyone's advice, including that of my own doctor who was on the Bellevue teaching staff, I refused to return upstate and went to Bellevue, prepared for the worst.

Bellevue Hospital rises, large and bleak, along New York's East River from 24th to 30th streets. I had begun to feel misgivings as soon as my husband and I came out of the subway on 23rd Street, and as we neared the hospital I clutched his hand. We stopped on First Avenue and looked at it across the traffic – dirty, red-brick buildings topped with green towers. I swallowed hard, trying to drive away the image I had always had of Bellevue as a public Bedlam, telling myself it was only another hospital. James set down my suitcase and stared at the buildings. Finally he said, "Italian Renaissance Revival – eclectic." I could have hit him.

James steered me through the main entrance into a long green waiting room. At one side was a high counter with cashiers' windows. Across from it were worn wooden benches, arranged in rows. Children ran between the rows, or crawled over old people huddled alone. Two Spanish families argued loudly; a drunk slept near them, ignoring the noise. A young woman in slacks stared at the ceiling, talking to herself.

James got directions from a clerk at one of the windows, and we turned right into a corridor at the far end of the room. Painted black arrows pointed the way to C and D Building: Chest Services. Interns strode purposefully by us. Waiting outpatients lined the benches along the walls; orderlies pushed stretchers past them. Ahead of us were three student nurses, radiant with starch – clean bright objects that seemed out of place in that dim corridor. We followed them, watching their little organdy caps bob with each rubber-soled step. They turned into a fluorescent-lighted lunchroom. James asked if I wanted some coffee. I shook my head. I wanted to get it over with.

The C and D admitting office turned out to be only another corridor, with a business niche at one end. A clerk motioned James and me to a bench while she examined my papers, and we sat down by an unshaven old man in a striped cotton bathrobe. He held his head in his hands, looking sick. Next to him sat a man in street clothes, one leg outstretched in a stained cast, brown toes protruding. We all looked past each other. On the wall above our bench, a sign read, first in English and then in Spanish:

> NOTICE: All persons admitted as patients to this hospital will be investigated financially. Patients or legally responsible relatives found able to pay for care will be required to do so.

This didn't apply to me, though. TB treatment is free – a good thing for us because we didn't have much money. James was teaching at Columbia, still working toward his Ph.D., and I had been a graduate student. My TB had come as a shock to both of us, and since

I had no idea that I had the disease until the symptoms became all too obvious, its progress was not easily checked. The only warning I had was that I seemed to be tired all the time. When I began to lose weight, I was delighted: I had always wanted interesting hollows below my round Ohio cheekbones. One afternoon, crossing the Columbia campus – it was summer and hot, the perfect cover for a constant 100-degree fever – I had to sit down on the library steps, suddenly too hot and tired to go to my Anglo-Saxon class. I sat on those steps feeling like a perfect fool, and then, despite the summer cold I couldn't seem to get rid of, I cut the class and went swimming in a Department of Parks outdoor pool. That night my "cold" became worse, and my coughing kept James awake. "Air pollution," I croaked.

In Anglo-Saxon class the next day, I was still coughing. I apologized to the boy who sat next to me and tried to laugh between spasms. "My twenty-sixth birthday is this week," I explained. I was thinking of Keats, who died of TB at that age, but the joke made me uncomfortable. That afternoon I went to the Columbia Health Service to get something for my cold and found that it wasn't a cold at all.

As James and I sat waiting, a wheeled stretcher, guided by orderlies, turned into the corridor and sped past us. On it were stained, rumpled sheets and clothing – a bloody shirt, gray pants with a leather belt still threaded through the loops. I looked at James. Something awful had happened to whoever had been wearing those clothes. For the first time, I was really frightened.

Finally the woman at the desk pointed to a door that said "Women's Bath" and told me to go in there and change. She gave me a white hospital gown that tied down the back, and a striped seersucker

Bellevue bathrobe. She said I could keep my shoes as slippers, and that I was to wear "this" over my mouth – it was a paper mask with string loops that went around the ears. I tried to smile at James, wondering how many people before me had worn that faded bathrobe, and if they'd ever left Bellevue afterward.

When I came out of the bathroom, carrying my own clothes, an elderly woman was waiting with a wheeled rack. She put a white cotton cover over my things and wheeled the rack away. Feeling helpless, I stood facing James in my Bellevue robe, the paper mask covering my mouth and nose. James grinned. "You look like an old lunger already." I handed him the little gold pin that had been on my suit collar, and he put it in his wallet. We sat and waited, silent and suddenly shy of each other. In a few minutes, a nurse's aide in a bright blue uniform arrived to take me upstairs. She handed me a paper bag for my belongings – no suitcases were allowed on the wards. James and I emptied my books and toilet articles into the bag, and I started to close the suitcase. "You can take your own pajamas," the nurse's aide said. "They only allows that on TB. It makes the girls look nicer. They stays so long, they like to have something colorful to wear once in a while."

I stuffed my pajamas and navy-blue wool robe into the paper bag and handed James the suitcase. Holding it, he gave me a hug with one arm. He looked young and pale standing there under the fluorescent lights. I followed the nurse's aide down the hall, wondering what I looked like from the back to James. I think we were both glad to get it over with.

There were two wards on the second floor of Chest Services, each with 45 to 50 female patients. The wards extended east and west from a bank of elevators and a recreation room. Each of the patients' rooms held six to twelve beds, and the upper halves of the walls between rooms were glass. It was possible to see through an entire ward just by sitting up in bed.

It was rest period – 1:00 to 2:30 in the afternoon – when the nurse's aide and I came off the elevator. I followed her, looking into dark rooms where the green blinds had been closed. The walls were painted that same institutional green, flaking toward the ceiling. The hall was dim, except for the light in the glassed-in nurses' station, and I could hear the rhythmic bellows of an iron lung rasping somewhere. Our footsteps echoed, and the quiet was riddled with spasms of coughing from the dark rooms. We stopped at the nurses' station, and I saw a uniformed policewoman seated on a wooden chair by its door, reading a magazine. My legs, cold and naked beneath the short gown, began to feel numb, and I curled my toes inside my loafers.

The aide handed my papers to a nurse, a heavy gray-haired woman who smiled in an automatic way and told me I could take off my mask now. I followed her down the corridor into one of the darkened rooms. There was an empty bed near the door. The blinds let in a gray-green light, and I could see heads rise from the other beds to look at me. The nurse put my paper bag on the shelf of a chipped gray-metal bedside stand. On top of the stand were a metal pitcher, a glass, a box of tissues, and a sputum cup. The nurse pressed the handle of the sputum cup and its metal lid flipped up to reveal a waxed-paper container. If I coughed, she told me, I was to cover my mouth with one of the tissues, and if I had to spit – she waved the cup under my nose – I was to spit only into this. She eyed me suspiciously, as if I might have been about to spit on the floor, and I decided it was useless to protest that I hadn't coughed for months. The nurse told me that one of the doctors would probably examine me that evening after supper. Then she stood waiting for me to get into bed. Smiling nervously, I took off my striped robe and my loafers. I kept feeling that one of us ought to be saying something reassuring. "Everything's going to be all right," I said. Trying to hold the short hospital gown down in back, I kneed myself onto the high bed and slid under the sheet. Looking satisfied, the nurse left. In the dark I saw five raised heads watching me. The nurse's steps echoed down the hall.

I reached over and pushed the sputum cup out of sight behind the metal pitcher. Then I turned my face to the wall and pulled the sheet over my ears.

That evening I was called to the examining room by one of the ward interns, a thin, dark young man, tired and cross. It was a general examination, hurried but thorough.

"You're here for surgery?" he said, lighting a cigarette.

I nodded. "How long will I have to stay?"

"All depends," he said. "Maybe a month, maybe longer. How's your Spanish?"

"I don't know any," I said.

"Too bad. Ninety-five percent of the patients on this floor are Spanish, or Negro, or both. They come up here from the south, and" – he snapped his fingers – "bingo!" He gave me a sleeping pill and watched while I swallowed it. "Well, good luck," he said.

The lights were already out when I got back to my room. I crawled into the high bed and lay listening to the murmur of Spanish and the muffled laughs. Footsteps echoed up and down the hall; somewhere the iron lung continued its gasping. I breathed shallowly, listening to the coughs and laughter cutting through the dark – and then the pill took over.

The next morning we had oatmeal. I was awakened by the food carts clinking in the hall and the smell of hot cereal. We lined up at the door to receive our trays and carried them back to our beds. No one said anything, and I ate in self-conscious silence, glancing around at my roommates. There were three beds facing me, three on my side of the room. In the bed directly across from mine sat a massive tan woman whom I had heard, during the night, speaking Spanish to the thin yellow-skinned woman in the bed next to hers. On the third bed, by the window, a small girl with thick black curls picked at her breakfast. Her mouth was bright pink, even without lipstick. There were two women in the other beds on my side of the room. The one near the window was elderly; the girl beside me seemed about my age, in her early twenties. Her hair was bushed out startlingly around her face, as if she had washed it and not got around to putting on straightener.

I had not met my roommates the afternoon before because they had gone off to a bingo game, run by the Bellevue Volunteers, in the 12-bed room next door. Now the bushy-haired girl raised her spoon, letting the oatmeal drip in globs. "Hi," she said. "How you like this place – ain't it the Ritz?"

Her name was Harriet, and she made introductions, waving her spoon around the room. "Juanita, Raquel. They don't speak much English. Marta Vasquez. Hey, Vasquez," she called to the girl pick-ing at her breakfast. "You eat that, hear? You got to get back your strength." The girl made a face, screwing up her pink mouth. "Marta had a baby last month," Harriet explained. "A little girl. And the doctors say she has got to get fat."

Marta made a distasteful noise into her oatmeal, which caused the two other Puerto Rican women to laugh.

"I am thee interpret," Marta announced suddenly. "I speak thee English good."

"Sure you do," Harriet snickered.

Marta looked at me. "I also speak thee *good* Spanish." She gestured disdainfully at the other Puerto Rican women and began chewing on a piece of jelly toast.

The older woman was Sarah; she had just come down from surgery after having had a whole lobe removed.

As we were finishing our coffee, the sputum-cup cart clanked in, pushed by two boys wearing white paper masks and orange rubber gloves. Harriet and Marta whipped out of bed and hurried to the window to confer with one of the boys. The other pushed the two-tiered cart next to Sarah's bed; they spoke in low tones and laughed. When the boy came to my bed, I showed him my cup. "It's clean," I said proudly.

"Doesn't matter." He replaced it with another. "Got your number?"

I stared.

"What's your number?" he repeated.

Holding the bedclothes around my waist, I scrabbled to the foot of the bed and peered over at the card that gave my name and religion. Jews had blue cards, Catholics yellow, and Protestants pink. I had said, "agnostic," and they had simply given me a pink card. There was no number on it. "I guess I haven't got one yet," I apologized.

"That's okay, honey." He winked above the white mask. "I'll be back tomorrow."

With a final wave of their orange gloves, the sputum-cup boys clanked off to the next room.

"Harriet," I said, "where do you get your number?"

"Well, I don't know – it just comes to me," Harriet said. "Like I get this feeling about it, you know. Vasquez over there, she always throws the dice, but it hasn't done her much – – " She saw my expression and burst out laughing. "Oh, oh, Lord! Hey, Vasquez! She want to know where she can get her number."

Marta gave off high, delighted giggles; Sarah cackled, then subsided into a fit of coughing.

This was my introduction to the Bellevue underground, a concern as private and as impressively organized as the Mafia. Its headquarters was somewhere in the depths of the hospital, and it functioned daily among the patients and certain nonprofessional members of the staff – the numbers racket. The agents for our building were the sputum-cup boys, who arrived each morning and exchanged much more than just sputum cups. It cost a dime to get in, Harriet explained, and you had to have a three-digit number. The winning number was revealed daily in the evening paper – the last three digits of the day's pari-mutuel take at some leading racetrack.

Harriet shook her head at me. "You are not going to *survive* this place," she said. "Right now you best come with me – the bathtub room's open." I took my basin from the stand, pulled my blue pajamas out of the paper bag, and followed Harriet down the hall.

The bathtub room was next to the bathroom. I had been introduced to the bathroom the night before. It had three toilets and two washbowls – for 45 of us. At bedtime it was jammed. Girls kept coughing in each other's faces and spitting in the washbowls, but they were only used for tooth-brushing anyway; no one in her right mind would have washed in those bowls. There were other washbowls on the ward, one by the door in each room, but we were told not to use these; they were for the doctors and nurses. We used them anyway. Every night before supper, the Puerto Rican girls would set covered glass jars in these bowls – rice and beans and chicken soup, brought in by friends during visiting hours – and run hot water over them for 15 to 20 minutes. The sound of running water was a regular dinner signal. Marta, Juanita, and Raquel lived almost entirely off these Puerto Rican CARE packages, eschewing the regular hospital fare. No one really minded about their cooking in these washbowls, just so long as they didn't *wash* in them. One was supposed to wash in the bathtub room, even though that was locked every evening at six.

That morning Harriet and I pushed our way through the heavy door and were met by a haze of steam and shouts for us to "Shut thee door!" It was a small square room crammed with girls in various stages of undress, noisy with multilingual chatter. A few girls stood around the single tub in the center of the room, waiting; the others made use of their water-filled basins. A scum of soapy water covered the tiles, so Harriet and I left our shoes by the door and sloshed our way across the floor. At my elbow, a round brown backside pivoted, a body straightened, and I saw a fox-brown face topped by an incredible head of orange hair. "Hey there," the girl said to Harriet. She looked me over, was not impressed, and deliberately returned her backside to my view. Harriet shook her head at me: "That bad Annie." We pushed our way to the washbowls and ran hot water into our basins. Some of Harriet's friends made floor space for her, but I was forced to fend for myself. When I had found a corner to set my basin in, I hung my gown and pajamas on a wall hook and went self-consciously about the business of washing. The bending, dipping bodies crowded around me made the room look like a seraglio scene in a low-budget movie.

Over someone's back, Harriet motioned for me to hurry. I dried myself, stepped into my pajamas, rolling the cuffs to keep them out of the water, and joined her. "This is Ruby," Harriet said. A tall, sunken-chested woman in a loose gray wrapper stood leaning against the wall, smoking a cigarette. She grinned down at me. "Ruby got the biggest feet in Bellevue," Harriet said. "Show her your feet, Ruby." I looked down; they were brown and flat, splayed out at the toes like swim fins. "Go on," Ruby said, shoving Harriet playfully. Ashes flickered down onto the milky tiles. Suddenly Ruby dropped her cigarette and covered her mouth. The cough racked her double, and she swayed forward. "Da-am," Harriet said. She took Ruby by the elbow, and we pushed our way to the door. "Ruby ain't supposed to be taking baths," Harriet explained. "She is sick, *sick*." She and the orange-haired Annie nudged Ruby through the door and down the hall, like tugboats flanking a listing ship. I followed, carrying the empty washbasins.

Soon after Harriet and I got back to our room, the doctors came in, making their morning rounds. There were three of them – the Chinese resident, Dr. Chan, and two interns. Behind them, carrying a clipboard, was the head nurse. The doctors began with Juanita and Raquel, so Marta fluttered over, showing her dimples and flirting, to act as "thee interpret."

Dr. Chan addressed the two women: "How do you feel today?"

Marta immediately transformed this into rapid, high-pitched Spanish sentences of great length. As she spoke, Juanita and Raquel broke into smiles and then snickers. Finally Juanita said something. Marta nodded and turned to Dr. Chan. "She say she want to go home. Thees place make her sick."

Dr. Chan gave up and turned away. Behind his back, Marta put both index fingers in her mouth and stretched her upper lip like a frog's.

The doctors moved on to Sarah and Harriet, then to me. "Mrs. Morris is here for surgery," Dr. Chan said to the interns. "She was a private patient of Dr. Smith's." I glanced at Harriet to see if she had heard him; something like that might ruin me socially.

Dr. Chan consulted his chart. "You'll go down to X-ray this afternoon."

"Thank you," I said stupidly.

When the doctors and the nurse had left, Harriet looked over at me. "You are going to have an operation?"

I nodded.

She looked sympathetic. "Je-sus! You seen the scars yet?"

I knew what she meant. Lung surgery is done from the back. The lung is entered by cutting a large, sickle-shaped flap extending, usually, from behind the shoulder and under the arm to just below the breast in front. Newly healed, the scar is not a pretty sight. I had seen them on girls in my old sanatorium.

I looked away and asked, "What happens next around here?"

"It's Friday," Harriet said. "Lord, we going to have macaroni again."

When I came back from X-ray that afternoon, the room was jammed. I could hear Juanita calling, "B-*cinco*. O-*sesenta y dos*." Spanish girls in bathrobes were sprawled over every bed, and the floor was littered with kernels of corn they were using as bingo-card markers. Marta and two friends, kneeling on her bed, were playing two cards each. Suddenly a plump teen-ager shrieked, "Beengo!" Juanita checked her card and gave her a water glass full of nickels. Then an empty glass was passed, into which everyone who wanted to play the next game had to drop a nickel for her card.

I got my knitting and backed into the corridor, which was empty except for the policewoman asleep in her chair. I wandered down past the elevators to the recreation room. Harriet was seated in a torn leather-and-metal-tubing chair, having her hair straightened by a girl whom she introduced as Mary. Several other girls were smoking and talking at a table by the window; a Puerto Rican woman was using the sewing machine. I found a chair and began knitting on the sleeve of the sweater I had begun upstate five months ago. The afternoon light, coming through the high narrow window, was gray. The room smelled of old cigarette butts and roach spray. I bent my head to hide my tears. I had been a hospital charity patient for eight months now. I wanted to go home – and I knew that I couldn't.

Juanita's bingo game, which went on night and day in our room, except for visiting hours, was nothing like the Tuesday-night bingo game run by the Bellevue Volunteers, whose prizes were just cakes of soap, toothpaste, and dental floss. Juanita's game was the real thing. It, and the numbers racket, provided the element of chance and disaster that was missing in our invalid lives.

Juanita was the ward matriarch and bossed the younger girls relentlessly; but they all respected her, saying she was a "very fine woman," often adding, "but ver-ry jealous." Later I discovered that she had seven children, and just before she arrived in Bellevue she had knifed her husband. He had been playing around. Luckily he hadn't died, but we all agreed that he probably wouldn't forget right away, either.

The policewomen on our ward weren't interested in Juanita. They were there mainly to keep an eye on the two dope addicts. There were three shifts of policewomen, and I felt sorry for the one who had to sit up all night on the hard wooden chair by the nurses' station. I felt even sorrier for the dope addicts, both of whom were in Ruby's and Mary's room. Except for being under arrest, they were disappointing. The younger one, Phyllis, didn't have any teeth on top, and it made her conversation lag. I tried to teach Phyllis to knit, but it was hard work because she was left-handed and because every night the police-woman took away her knitting needles until morning.

None of us liked the morning policewoman. She was heavy-set, lethargic, and mean-looking. Harriet's friend Annie thought she was a Lesbian because she accompanied the poor addicts to the bathtub room. In there, Annie would swagger back and forth, insolently shaking her backside, hoping that the policewoman would give herself away. This performance would break up Harriet and Ruby. "How come you so irresistible, Annie?" they would tease. "You best retire. Can't even give it away." The policewoman seemed bored with the whole routine.

Evening visiting hours were Mondays, Wednesdays, and Fridays from 7:00 to 8:00, and this was Friday. Marta began getting ready right after supper. First she carefully washed out the Mason jar that held her evening meal of rice and beans. All through supper, Harriet and I had yelled at her that she was a spoiled brat for not eating the food on her tray, and by 6:00 she was no longer speaking to us. At 6:15, humming loudly, she put on a pair of black silk stockings, smoothing them over her legs under the short white hospital gown. Then she changed her earrings, substituting long jet dangles for her everyday gold loops. At 6:30 she produced an array of cosmetic jars and bottles and began to do her face, singing in Spanish. By 7:00, we could barely recognize her. Her lips gleamed gelatinously red, her nails were scarlet to the cuticle, and she had outlined her eyes with mascara until she resembled a small, vampish raccoon.

Neither Harriet nor I was expecting anyone. James had made arrangements to take his Ph.D. orals at Columbia soon, and we had an understanding that he would visit only twice a week until they were over. Harriet seldom had visitors. Occasionally her parents or a girlfriend came by, but she had been in Bellevue for four months – people stop coming after so much time. Harriet was divorced, and her 10-year-old son, Benny, lived with her parents in Harlem. It distressed her that Benny was back in Harlem. She had tried for many years to leave and had finally found an apartment in a project on the Lower West Side. When she became ill, she lost the apartment, and

Benny had to change schools. Harriet's parents were elderly, and she was afraid Benny would get in with one of the bad gangs back in the old neighborhood.

Marta began prancing about the room, much to the amusement of Juanita and Raquel as they left to listen to their favorite Spanish soap opera on the radio in Room 27.

"*Amor, amor, che che che*," sang Marta, fluttering her artificial eyelashes. Harriet and I could have strangled her. Certainly we did not need to be reminded that Julio was coming; he never missed a visiting night.

Marta and Julio had been married for three months. The social worker on our floor, a gentle white-haired woman who seemed totally untouched by reality, had arranged the wedding in a Bellevue chapel a few weeks after Marta landed in the hospital, consumptive and seven months pregnant. Juanita and Julio's cousin had served as witnesses. I don't think getting formally married had occurred to Marta. Julio had been her faithful common-law husband for over a year, but he had to buy her a ring, and she liked that. Her baby had been taken to a foundling home when it was a week old; now it had as much reality for her as the cherubs in Juanita's prayer book.

At seven promptly, Julio arrived. His curly hair was slicked down, and he wore a blue suit with a red bow tie. He carried a bakery box and a bouquet of small roses and daisies. Marta dragged him possessively to her corner. With great show, she arranged the flowers in her water pitcher. She opened the bakery box, exclaiming, and set a small white cake on her bed tray. The frosting shone moistly through shaggy coconut, and I heard Harriet swallow. The fish we had had for supper had been dry, but we had eaten it to provide a good example for Marta.

Sarah was visiting down the hall, and soon Marta and Julio were seated side by side on Marta's bed, oblivious of Harriet and me. The room became electric with their pinings. Harriet grabbed my arm. "C'mon," she said.

We walked down the hall, peering into various rooms to see if any of Harriet's friends had gotten anything good to eat. No one beckoned to us. We passed the elevators, full of gloom. "I'd give anything to go to a restaurant again," Harriet said. "Every Friday, after work, Benny and me used to eat at the Chinese restaurant. Sweet and sour pork, chicken with – – "

"Stop it," I said.

Harriet's eyes widened as she looked at the pay telephone. "Hey, why not?"

Going through the Yellow Pages, we found a Chinese restaurant near Bellevue. Harriet dropped a dime in the phone and dialed. "Do you deliver… ?"

By 8:30, all the visitors had left except Julio, who was clinging to Marta by the elevators. Harriet sat waiting inside the phone booth and I straddled a chair beside it; when a Chinese boy emerged from an elevator, carrying a large brown paper bag, we fell upon him with cries. We paid him and carried the bag past Marta, making sure that she got a whiff of the egg rolls and sweet-and-sour pork.

The ward lights were turned off at nine, so we took the rest of our egg-rolls under our robes to the bathroom, going separately so as not to arouse suspicion. Annie and Ruby were already there, eating barbecued pork chops and fried plantain that Annie's visitors had brought. The air was a stifling combination of barbecue sauce, Lysol, and cigarette smoke. Harriet and I traded two of our egg rolls for a pork chop. Ruby passed around a quart bottle of warm, foamy root beer. I knew that Ruby was horribly contagious and that I was not, but I took a swallow, praying that the TB drugs we took were on the job. We ate greedily, wiping our greasy fingers on toilet paper. Then we all had cigarettes out of Annie's pack and smoked a lot.

By the time we got back to the room, Marta had decided to be friends again and gave us pieces of her cake to make amends. The three of us sat on my bed in the dark, spilling shreds of coconut on the sheets, and Marta decided to tell the story of her life – "so you will know how I have suffered."

"Don't talk with your mouth full," Harriet said.

"I have been born in Puerto Rico," Marta told us seriously. "My mother is dead, and my grandmother has raised me. I have thee good education from thee Sisters, but" – her eyes grew solemn, and she sighed – "I am married when I am fifteen years old. To an old man. Thirty-three years!"

Harriet and I listened, licking icing from our fingers.

Marta's husband had taken her to New York, and he had grown very mean. After seven months, she had received a letter from Puerto Rico saying that her grandmother was dead. This had made her very sad. And her husband was cruel. He stopped going to work. He would leave home for days at a time. Marta was afraid. She did not like New York, and she didn't speak "thee English" then. When her husband *was* home, he beat her. One day she found "thee needle and thee powder" under their mattress and became frightened and ran away. She hid all night in the park, under some bushes. In the morning, she went to the family of her husband's uncle, and they took her in, but – Marta shook her head – the uncle tried to do bad things to her, and she was always afraid that her husband might find her. Then she had met Julio Vasquez. Julio was 25 years old and had "thee good job." She had gone home with him. Now she was 17 years old.

Harriet and I listened to this story with dismay. Marta had never been divorced from her husband. I thought wickedly how that would put the social worker's nose out of joint.

"But now I speak thee English. Everything is good," Marta concluded proudly. "Julio is father – and I, I am thee mother."

Several mornings later, Harriet woke me by shaking my shoulder. The room was dark. "I'm going to give you your gastric," she said.

"What?" Blinking, I lifted my head.

"Hush, you going to wake the ward." Harriet switched on the little light clipped to the bedstead. The bulb threw a pale circle onto my pillow.

Harriet was holding a kidney-shaped basin. In it lay a coiled orange rubber catheter and a small glass cylinder with a plunger at one end. She poured a glass of water from my pitcher. I looked around the room. Marta's bed was empty. Everyone else was asleep.

"We got to hurry," Harriet said. "I got eight more of these to do."

"What do you mean, *you*?"

I had had gastrics before and they are not pleasant. A sample of gastric fluid is drawn from the stomach early in the morning. The sample is then placed in a Petri dish, and a culture is grown to see if tuberculosis bacilli develop. If they do, the patient is considered infectious, or "positive" – the disease is not yet arrested. In my previous sanatorium, the gastrics had been done by the doctor or the head nurse.

"Are you crazy?" I said.

Harriet looked hurt. "Honey, you don't want them interns messing up your insides. They never done this before. I done fourteen last month."

She was right; we had a new set of interns. "But who said for *you* to?" I protested. "Where's the nurse?"

"Don't be dumb." She looked at me pityingly. "You supposed to do it yourself. Marta and I does it for the new girls because *we* are the *best*. We don't get it done before the interns come, they going to do it for you."

I could hear Marta singing to herself outside in the hall. "*Amor, che che, amor…* " She stopped at the door, carrying a basin, and looked in at Harriet. "Thee third," she said triumphantly, and went on down the hall.

"She's good," Harriet admitted grudgingly, "but she ain't got the light touch. You ready?"

"Oh, God," I said.

Harriet handed me the rubber tube, and I inserted it in my right nostril. Closing my eyes, I began pushing it through. I stopped. "How can you tell when I hit bottom?"

"Je-sus," Harriet said, "you ain't going to sur-vive this place. Now swallow." She held out the glass of water. I could feel the tube against the back of my throat; now I gulped some air and began drinking furiously. The water and the contractions carried the tube down past my glottis. I felt as if I might be going to choke.

"Swallow." Harriet poured more water into my glass. "Swallow, dammit!"

I felt the tube trail safely down inside; I hadn't strangled. I watched Harriet's brown hands as she held up the remaining length. "That look good. We'll try." She fitted the glass cylinder onto the tube and slowly pulled out the plunger. There was a bubbling sound, and the tube began to fill with an opaque yellow liquid. "Here." Harriet handed me the cylinder. "You want to try?"

I drew the plunger carefully, feeling a scraping in my stomach, and the tube filled. "That fine," Harriet said. She unfastened the cylinder and corked it. Then she took the dangling end of the tube in her hand. "Ready?" I nodded and exhaled, and she drew the tube up and out in one smooth motion. She penciled my name on the adhesive tape about the cylinder. "You ain't so bad," she said. "Now I got to do that Mary, and she a real sissy."

When James arrived that evening, I greeted him proudly. "Guess what? I pumped my own stomach today."

James looked sick.

"Think what a hit I'll be at faculty parties," I joked, and then I realized that his disgust was genuine. I looked around the gray-green room, at the narrow beds, at my friends slouching around in faded Bellevue robes or flimsy wrappers.

I looked at James defiantly. "I'm very good at it," I said. "One of the best." From that time on I was.

The last week in March a notice appeared on the bulletin board by the nurses' station. Some folk singers from Greenwich Village had volunteered to come to Bellevue to entertain the patients. Everyone began looking forward to it; it was something to do.

The morning of the day the singers were to arrive, Elena was released from the psychiatric building. Elena was the girl who had had my bed before I arrived. My friends described her as a "very sweet girl, but very ner-vous." She had been on the ward for five months, and then one day she threatened to jump out the widow. Dr. Chan and finally half the ward had come running. In the commotion, Elena, hysterical, broke Dr. Chan's glasses. She had been taken off to the psychiatric building in a strait jacket, still covered with blood from Dr. Chan's nose, and not heard of since.

The doctors were worried about people committing suicide, Harriet told me, so Elena should have known better. Only a month before, an old man upstairs had jumped out the window. He had been a terminal lung-cancer patient; still, the doctors were understandably nervous about everyone.

The day of the folk singers' concert Elena came back, looking fine, to say good-bye. She was being sent home because her disease had been arrested by drugs, and she could be treated as an outpatient. In keeping with tradition, she gave away all her hospital things to the girls who had to remain. She gave her pink flannel robe with lace on the collar to Raquel, who didn't have a robe of her own. Marta and Harriet got her bingo prizes – soap and dental floss – and she bequeathed to our whole room her expensive atomizer bottle of perfume.

The evening concert was to be held downstairs in one of the medical lecture rooms, and although limited to TB patients, it was going to be mixed. We would get a chance to have a look at the male patients. By 7:30 we had all assembled at the elevators. Every girl who had her own bathrobe was wearing it. The Puerto Rican girls were dazzling – some wore high heels with their pajamas and enough makeup to compensate for the days when there hadn't been any point in wearing it. We all smelled like Spanish *majas*; Elena's atomizer bottle had made the rounds.

Our first disappointment came soon. Seated on the platform of the lecture room were four of the sloppiest-looking young people I had ever seen. The boys were bearded and wore T-shirts, faded jeans, and sandals. The girls wore no makeup, and they were dressed in black turtleneck sweaters. Long, limp hair spilled about their shoulders. Since we had worn our best for them, it seemed bad manners that they had not done the same. We had not been expecting the Rockettes, but a few sequins would have cheered us. As the male patients filed in, our disappointment grew. TB's male victims are often undernourished, alcoholic Bowery types, and this fact was obvious now. Many of the men had not even bothered to shave. They looked awful.

The singers introduced themselves by their first names, then strummed their guitars into the opening selection. We couldn't make out all the words, but it seemed to be an injunction for us all to escape slavery and take the underground railway "North to Freedom!" After this they played several work songs, a prison lament, and some I.W.W. ballads. They stood before us, young and earnest, singing in well-bred mid-western voices, sincerely identifying with us – the poor, the downtrodden, the socially oppressed masses. We were bored stiff; what we had come to see was a little high life. Most of the old men wandered off, but we stayed out of good manners, conscious of being hostesses. It was, after all, *our* hospital. The young singers finished with a medley of spirituals in which they invited us to join. No one did. After a moment of limply polite applause, we were glad to file out.

Going down the hall, I said to Ruby, "What did you think of it?"

"They call *that* entertainment?" Ruby said in disgust. "Hell, they ain't even wearing shoes!" Her enormous feet, in scuffs, slapped against the tiles. "Why didn't they sing something new? Singing about them old cotton fields. Don't they know how *old* that is?"

Harriet came up to us, and Ruby nudged her. "We going to see a little action now." I wondered what was up.

Soon after the lights went out that night, Harriett got up and put on her robe. "Follow me in a couple of minutes, and bring your glass," she whispered. "Marta going to follow you."

When I got to the bathroom, Annie, Ruby, and Mary were there with Harriet. Two Puerto Rican girls were talking to each other from within the toilet cubicles, and Ruby stood leaning against a basin, silent, her arms crossed over her chest. "What's up?" I asked, and Harriet shook her head in warning. Marta slipped into the room, tittering with excitement. "Thee roses... " she began, and Harriet shut her up. At last, the Puerto Rican girls left.

Grinning, Ruby uncrossed her arms and pulled a gurgling fifth of Four Roses whiskey from under her robe. "Happy Birthday, Ruby," she said. "We going to have a party!"

Everyone laughed. We brought out our water glasses, and Ruby poured us large, musical dollops.

Annie held her glass up to the light so that the amber whiskey flashed. "Uh… many happy returns to Ruby."

We clinked glasses and took big swallows. Marta gasped. I don't think she had ever tasted whiskey before. "Roses… ?" she said doubtfully.

Mary toasted Ruby's brother, who had brought the bottle, and we drank again. When Annie produced a bag of cheese twists, we toasted her. Then, at Marta's suggestion, we toasted Dr. Chan, who must have been sleeping uneasily at that moment. By the time we emptied the bottle, Marta was no longer speaking "thee good English," or even "thee good Spanish." She giggled charmingly as she began to slide down a wall.

The party was over. Ruby carefully smashed the empty whiskey bottle inside a towel and flushed the fragments down the toilet. Then Harriet and I took hold of Marta and rushed her down the hall. There were no nurses in sight; the policewoman was asleep in her chair. It was just after midnight.

The next morning, while Harriet and I were helping the nurse's aides change our beds, I was told Dr. Chan wanted to see me.

In the examining room, Dr. Chan looked up from his charts and smiled. The smile looked sinister to me. "Ah, Mrs. Morris," he said. "Yes. Sit down." I sat on the edge of a wooden chair, smoothing my bathrobe over my knees. Dr. Chan leaned back. "Mrs. Morris, we are both educated people."

Oh God! I thought. Something awful has happened in my X-ray.

Dr. Chan looked straight at me. "There have been infraction in the hospital rule. I have need to know who is breaking these rule. I know you are educated person like myself, but you have friends of the patients. I have discovered that there is *drinking*" – his eyes narrowed as he pronounced the word – "in the hospital. I have need to know who has been bringing *whiskey* into the hospital – on this floor."

I stared back at him. I had been pleased that my friends had trusted me enough to invite me to the party. This was a ghetto; I was one of them. And I was happier in Bellevue than I had been all the long months upstate. "What whiskey?" I said.

At the end of that week, though my operation was not scheduled for several days, I was transferred to the fifth-floor surgery ward.

The night before my operation James came to see me. He sat beside the bed, and I held up my wrist to show him the strip of clear plastic that circled it. Inside the plastic, my name was written on a strip of paper. "Look, James."

He said lightly, "That's in case they misplace you tomorrow, before you come to."

I looked at him squarely. "It's for the morgue. In case they make a mistake. In case nobody claims me."

"Nonsense," James said, grinning. "I'd claim you."

Miss Cooper, the practical nurse, appeared to remind him that he would have to leave soon so that she could "prepare me." The phrase amused James, but it made me feel helpless.

"James," I said. "I'm scared."

"Yes, I know." His eyes were worried; they pleaded with me not to blame him, not to ask him for help.

"It isn't fair," I said.

"Try not to think of it that way." He got up to leave, and I walked him down the hall to the elevators.

"Be good," he said. "Don't frighten the doctors." His hand was sweaty, and he kissed me on the forehead.

Miss Cooper was waiting beside my bed with a basin of water, a safety razor, and a bottle of liquid soap. "I've got to prepare your back," she said. "Then you can see your clergyman."

"I don't need a clergyman," I said.

"It's customary, before a major operation, to be visited by a clergyman of your faith." Miss Cooper's eyes narrowed. "Your card says Protestant."

"I don't want to see a minister," I said.

"You can see a priest or a rabbi."

"I don't want to see anybody," I repeated.

She kept looking at me. "How do you know you won't be sorry?"

"I won't know," I said.

She shaved my back, then painted it with antiseptic. "Have you changed your mind?"

I pressed my forehead into the pillow. "I don't think so."

After Miss Cooper left, Dr. Bennett came in. Dr. Bennett was a resident, specializing in lung surgery. Bellevue is essentially a teaching hospital – it was staffed by the Columbia and New York University medical schools – and my operation would be a teaching demonstration. It was to be a simple segmental resection, a removal of about one eighth of my right lung. "The superior segment of the lower lobe," the doctor said. "About the size of your fist."

I made a fist and looked at it.

"Do you know you're very lucky?" he said. "Not so many years ago, this operation couldn't even be done."

"If I were lucky, I wouldn't need it," I said.

After the doctor left, I carefully put up my long hair as usual, not sure why I was doing it. Then the night-medication cart came around, and there was a sleeping pill on it for me.

Very early in the morning, while it was still dark, the night nurse woke me. She had a needle to give me before she went off duty. "This will help you relax," she said.

I walked quietly past my sleeping roommates and down the empty hall to the bathroom. I opened the frosted window and leaned out, looking across the black East River, breathing the gray early air. The Sunshine Biscuit sign across the river was visible through the lifting smog. I breathed as deeply as I could, feeling sentimental about my lung; then I went to the washbowl, brushed my teeth, and unpinned my hair. I was beginning to get dizzy. When I got back to my room, I had trouble crawling up onto the bed.

Soon a strange nurse wheeled in a stretcher and asked if I was ready. I crawled awkwardly onto the stretcher and the nurse fastened a white cap over my hair. I lay flat, and we wheeled down the hall, past the nurses' station, and along the corridor.

Behind me the nurse said, "I hear you refused to see a clergyman."

I looked up and back at her upside-down face. She was young.

"Yes," I said.

"If you want to change your mind, there's still time."

I watched the paint-chipped ceiling passing overhead. The ceiling changed. We entered the operating room and the stretcher stopped under flat, round lights. A man in a green gown, cap, and mask leaned over me.

"This is Dr. Irwin, your anesthetist," the nurse said as they slid me from the stretcher onto the operating table. "We're going to put you to sleep now."

I felt a needle enter my arm and began counting. Overhead, the lights broke into dazzling grains of black and white. The grains sifted and the light sparkled – it was like being close to a movie screen. I continued counting. The glitter fuzzed black and diminished inward toward a tiny retreating light.

When I opened my eyes again, I saw James. I was back in the room and there seemed to be a light shining behind my bed. I became aware of heat and pain. I closed my eyes and tried to go back, but oxygen was being forced down my throat through a thin tube inserted into one nostril.

James leaned over. "Anne?"

I had to get that tube out of my throat. I raised my arm to pull at it, and pain splashed in my chest.

"Anne, don't," James said.

I tried again with my left arm. Something pulled sharply at the soft inner flesh; above me a plasma bottle rocked on its slender aluminum rod.

"Stop it," James said, scared.

I lay unable to move, drenched with perspiration, beginning to feel the tight layers of adhesive tape jacketing my chest and shoulder. I realized that I was lying on my incision and wondered if I should be. The sound of air bubbling through a water pump filled my head, and I looked down at my side. The tube was there, as Dr. Bennett had explained it would be – protruding, held in place by strips of tape, trailing out from under my hospital gown and over the side of the bed to the suction pump.

The tube was to draw out the air escaping into the space between my lung and chest wall. If it were not constantly pumped out, the pressure around the lung would become greater than that inside it, and the lung would collapse like a deflated balloon. The bubbling sound was my own drawn-out breath passing through the water bottles in which the pump's vacuum was created.

What Dr. Bennett had not explained was how it would feel. My chest seemed to have congealed into a solid weight that forced the curved incision down into the bed; as I breathed, the flesh around the freshly punctured hole in my side sucked rawly against the tube.

I tried to call out to James, but exhaled only a dry sound. To my left something moved. I turned my head and saw the ward nurse above me, smiling at James. She was a bosomy woman; her white nylon front rose and fell as she bent to tie my good arm to a flat, padded board. Then she swabbed the arm and inserted a hypodermic needle. Above me, James's mouth went slack. He hated needles, but he held my hand until I passed out...

The room was early-morning dark, and the night nurse's aide had switched on the tall gooseneck lamp with its metal hood. The bubbling noise of my breath passing through the water bottles followed me out of sleep.

"Here." The nurse's aid held out a rope made from a torn sheet. "Set up."

I inhaled. The tube was gone from my throat; the plasma bottle had disappeared.

The nurse's aide pushed the cloth rope at me. "You got to use your arm."

With my good arm, I picked up my dead arm by the wrist and lifted it to the rope. The fingers gripped.

"I'll give you a start," she said, cranking the bed. The upper half of the mattress rose, and I could see that the rope was tied to the foot of the bed.

"You supposed to pull yourself up."

I tried to tell her I couldn't move, but my voice rasped. She was holding a metal washbasin.

"Go on. You got to move, or you'll get adhesions." I shook my head.

"Set up," she said, coming closer. I remembered that we did not like her. She put the basin on the bedstand and advanced toward my head.

"I got to wash you," she said. "Hurry up." She took my arm near the taped shoulder, and pulled.

The arm wrenched me forward, lifting me. I opened my mouth to scream and clutched the rope, shaking. As my head fell forward, I was nauseated with pain and vomited over her hand.

She let go quickly. "Damn you!"

I fell back hard, on top of my stitches, and burned.

After two weeks, I had begun to feel that the water bottles were an extension of my body. Each time a tube was removed the lung slowly collapsed, and a new tube had to be inserted into my anesthetized chest with a painful, fleshy crunch. I was becoming an embarrassment to the young doctors. They were doing exactly as they had been taught; it seemed to them an obstinacy on my part that my lung refused to cooperate. We kept apologizing to each other. Between injections I lay helpless, steeped in narcotic sweat, unable to eat.

My roommates – Clara Rosado, Catalina Jiménez, Lucia Ortiz – were quite ashamed of me because I was not "ver-ry brave," but they brought and emptied bedpans anyway. There was an understanding in the room about that; there were never enough nurses.

The four of us were the only patients left on the chest-surgery ward, the last operations till fall. Only emergencies were performed during the summer because of the heat. Clara was recuperating from her operation. Lucia and Catalina were scheduled soon.

Catalina was terrified. She had arrived on Five clutching a paper

68

bag filled with her belongings, her black eyes round and wet with fear, submitting only because her husband had ordered her to.

Lucia Ortiz wasn't worried at all. She was older than the rest of us. We were all in our 20s; Lucia was, in her own words, "a girl of forty." She was short and squat, and her round head was pulled permanently off-center to the right. As if to offset this, she had been born with a walleye looking in the other direction. She was forever waddling up to my bed in friendship and then coughing in my face. One evening I opened my eyes, aware of some presence, and saw a small pink octopus dangling from a fork before my mouth. Lucia was offering it to me, a delicacy her mother had brought her. She was lucky that I had developed laryngitis and couldn't scream. During the second week that my lung kept collapsing and collapsing, Lucia had her operation, healed in three days, and had her tubes removed.

Finally my lung stopped collapsing. The last tube was pulled out, and I was no longer umbilically attached to those murmuring bottles. The fever subsided. My ribs still ached and my arm hung nearly useless, but it was over. I had believed that it might never end, and it had only been two weeks.

The day after the tube went, the occupational therapist looped strips of sheeting over the rods that haloed Lucia's bed and mine, making nooses for our wrists, and showed us how to raise our dead arms by pulling the other end of the strip. Lucia and I sat for hours, jerking our marionette arms up and down to exercise them.

The afternoon before Catalina's operation – it was a lobectomy, the removal of an entire lobe – Mr. Jiménez brought their little boy to the parking lot so that she could see him. It was raining, but we all leaned out of the window, getting wet, waving down five stories to where "thee little boy" stood holding his father's hand under a round black umbrella.

Dr. Bennett had tried to explain about the lobectomy, but Catalina could not understand him. She was taken to surgery the next morning, terrified and confused.

We waited restlessly. The air was heavy, and we could not open the window because it was raining. About noon, Catalina's bed came rattling down the hall. Catalina lay in it, still unconscious. A nurse ran beside the bed, guiding the wheeled pole with the transfusion bottle rocking on top, feeding blood into Catalina's arm. Another nurse dragged the rack with the pressure bottles attached to the tube in Catalina's left side. The bed was rolled into our room, and Dr. Bennett started the bottles pumping air out of her chest. An oxygen tank was ready; now its tube was inserted through a waxy nostril. The doctor went away, leaving the Puerto Rican practical nurse in charge.

That evening Mr. Jiménez, a Disciple of Christ, and seven other Disciples came to pray over Catalina. The six men and two women stood around her bed, praying aloud in Spanish. Catalina lay helpless, her fevered eyes shining, looking up from one bowed face to another with the trusting expression of a sacrificial pet.

Catalina had two tubes in her narrow chest, pumping constantly for six days. The flesh above her left breast, where the rib sections had been removed, sank into a yellow hollow you could put your fist in. In her pain and fever, she kept pointing to the hole, not understanding how it had gotten there. Clara and I took turns staying awake those long nights in case she needed water or the bedpan. We knew the night nurse had two floors to watch that week.

Mr. Jiménez came every evening and prayed aloud, holding her hand, until the tubes were removed.

One morning a week later, Clara was leaning out of the window in our room, moping in the early sun. The weather had turned warm again after weeks of rain, and the sky was bright blue. Below, on 26th Street, student nurses crossed back and forth from the nursing-school residence. Occasionally an ambulance would come sirening up to the Bellevue emergency entrance. Suddenly Clara leaned far out, looking right. "*Mira!*" she shrieked. "*Mira, mira!*"

I ran to the window.

Coming east on 26th Street were five elephants, walking in a swaying line, trunk to tail like a picture book. The sun beamed on their powdery backs, and their ears waved slowly like oars.

"Elephants!" I said. "El-e-phants! Good God, those are *elephants!*"

The line moved steadily down the street. Catalina asked to see. She was trying to get out of bed, and Clara and I ran to help her to the window. Perspiration stood out above her black brows.

The three of us leaned out. "Ah," Catalina said. "I have never seen. I can tell thee little boy."

Our faces grew warm in the sun as we watched the elephants' slow procession. Two men ran beside them now with long prods.

Behind us Mrs. Cohn, the ward nurse, said, "They come here every spring. For more than fifty years Ringling Brothers has come to Bellevue."

Catalina was sagging, and we helped her back into bed. Her hands made gestures above the sheet. "Thee little boy, he love thee animal," she explained. "He has never seen, but he have thee animal book."

Mrs. Cohn said that Clara, Lucia, and I had permission to go to the circus. It was to be held at 10:00 that morning in the court behind the administration building. She told us to sit with the second-floor tuberculosis patients and gave us white paper masks to wear.

When Mrs. Cohn left, Catalina turned hurt eyes on us. "Oh," she whispered. "I have never seen."

Clara looked at me unhappily. "If we had a wheel-chair... " I

71

said, and she nodded. We knew there were lots of old wheelchairs in the supply room.

We waited until Lucia had gone to join the second-floor girls; we were afraid she might tell on us. Then I kept watch while Clara stole a huge oak chair with enormous wheels. We rolled it quickly to our room and helped Catalina into it. We put my navy-blue wool robe on her, wrapped a blanket around her knees, and Clara stuffed a pillow behind her back so she wouldn't be jarred if we hit a bump. Catalina was gasping now, but she smiled at us. "I can tell thee little boy," she said.

I slipped into a Bellevue robe, and we wheeled Catalina out into the hall. We were halfway to the elevator when Dr. Bennett turned onto the corridor – we almost ran him down. He stood looking at the three of us. Catalina had closed her eyes in fright; her face was shiny with sweat, and she had begun to lean to the side.

"Do you know that child has a temperature of one hundred and three?" Dr. Bennett said finally. He started off with the chair, then looked back over his shoulder at Clara and me. "You two better get going," he said. "Before I lose my temper – and my job."

We ran toward the elevators.

The main-floor corridor was crowded with patients. Student nurses and blue-smocked Bellevue volunteers led groups of bandaged children. Wheelchairs were hurried along by orderlies. Men and women hobbled forward on crutches. It was like the evacuation of the wounded after a major battle.

Clara and I made our way with the steadily moving throng. At the door leading to the court, nurse's aides were distributing blankets for the patients to wrap around their shoulders.

Outside, we stood blinking in the bright sunlight. A brass band was playing marches, and we could see the elephants in a semicircle behind an improvised ring. Bleachers had been set up facing the East River, and we saw the TB patients seated together, their paper masks making them look like an organized cheering section. We pushed toward them, trailing our blankets. It felt strange to be outdoors again.

Annie, Marta, and Ruby were waving to us. We worked our way through the wheelchairs in front of the bleachers, and climbed to seats beside our friends. "Where's Harriet?" I asked.

They all looked uncomfortable. Finally Annie said, "She sign herself out. She say to tell you good-bye."

Ruby explained that Harriet had gotten a phone call last week. Her 10-year-old son, Benny, was in trouble with the police. He and some other boys had been caught breaking into a penny gum machine in front of a store on Lenox Avenue. Harriet had called a lawyer and signed herself out that afternoon. Dr. Chan had been furious, and the girls were worried because no one had thought to get her address. "But she has got her duty," Ruby said. "I going to miss her. Maybe she come to visit. She going to get her pills at the clinic." I asked if Harriet would have to go back to work; we all knew that might cause a relapse. "Maybe she get relief," Annie said hopefully, but Ruby sighed. "Naw, they just send her back here. She has got her problems."

Clowns with oversized papier-mâché heads were cavorting in the ring. One clown was dressed as a doctor, the other wore a nurse's cap. Both carried enormous painted-plywood surgical instruments. After a brassy fanfare, six tumblers in purple tights bounded out, somersaulting to a rendition of "The Daring Young Man on the Flying Trapeze." Behind them, we could see the platforms for the highwire act being secured and some little zebras, shying and backstepping on narrow black hoofs. The blue sky stretched far over the East River, silhouetting the wire walkers and the factories in Queens.

Now the animals entered the ring and circled daintily, athletic women in spangled tutus high-stepping beside them. The llamas' matted white necks thrust forward as they trotted around and their long lashes blinked at us. Clowns dashed in and out of the ring, bumping into one another, then recoiling in mock horror. The elephants stood upright on little stools, waving their gray trunks against the bright sky. The music waltzed and blared. We did not want it to end.

Clara and I stayed out in the courtyard long after the band had gone. We had slipped off our masks so we wouldn't be made to go back upstairs with the other TB patients, and we sat in the wooden bleachers, letting the sun warm our faces, breathing deeply in spite of our sore ribs, until finally we were chased inside.

When we got back on the ward we were late for lunch and Mrs. Cohn was irritated. We ate our cold tomato soup, still dazzled by the sunlight and music. Then Lucia and I sang the "Flying Trapeze" song for Catalina while Clara high-stepped around the beds, waving an aluminum water pitcher above her head.

The Sunday morning after the circus I was released from Bellevue. Wearing my street clothes, unfamiliar now and too large, I was ready by the time James arrived to take me home. He had brought a suitcase, but there was very little to carry because, in the Bellevue tradition, I had given all my hospital things away. After almost a year of hospitals, I was going home.

Clara and Lucia walked me to the elevators, where we met Annie and Marta, who had sneaked upstairs to say good-bye. We all stood there, awkward and sad, embarrassed in front of James. When the elevator came we hugged each other roughly, spreading germs, and then James and I got into the elevator. We were all crying when the metal doors creaked closed: the other girls because they had to stay; I because it was the end of something – and now I was a little afraid of what might be outside.

THE GOOD HUMOR MAN

ALL THROUGH THAT HOT, SLOW SUMMER, I lived alone, on ice-cream sandwiches and gin, in a one-room apartment on Carmine Street, waiting while James divorced me. In June he sent a letter saying, "Dear Anne, I have gone West to get the divorce." I was not sure where he meant by "West" and I did not believe he could just do that, without me, until I noticed that he had used the definite article. James was an English instructor at Columbia, and his grammar was always precise. So I knew that he could. The letter arrived two days before graduation. I remember taking it from the mailbox as I left the apartment, stopping just inside the shadow of the doorway to open it. Outside, the sun glanced off Carmine Street and rose in waves of heat, assaulting the unemptied garbage cans by the stoop. For the past week I had been planning to go to graduation. I wanted to see James walk in the academic procession as a member of the faculty, wearing a cap and gown. When the pain struck, I also felt a childish chagrin at having been disappointed.

For the past year, everything had gone badly with us, and James had wanted a separation. He had met someone else. I didn't want him to leave, and for months I alternated between anger and tears. With each new outburst, he became more determined. I never meant to throw his copy of Milton out the window. Finally, just after Christmas, James left, packing his share of our belongings. I didn't know where he had moved to; he wouldn't tell me. I put the rest – one-half of everything – in storage and sublet a small walkup in the South Village. I still wanted to see James, though I knew there was someone else, and I began to search for him. He did not want to encounter me; he hated scenes. That winter and spring, I pursued James through the cold, crowded streets of New York like an incompetent sleuth. What I remember of those sad months merges into one speeded-up sequence, as silent and jumpy as an old movie.

It started one January afternoon, chilly and gray. I was wearing a trenchcoat and scarf. Rain blew in on me where I stood, in the doorway of the Chinese laundry on Amsterdam Avenue. My bangs were dripping down onto my dark glasses, so that I could scarcely see who got off the No. 11 bus opposite Columbia. I was coming down with a damn cold. Inside, the Chinaman could be seen talking rapidly to his wife. He pointed repeatedly to me and then to his watch.

In February, I spotted James leaving Butler Library. He glanced nervously over his shoulder. Four girls in scarves and trenchcoats were approaching from various directions of the campus; they were converging on the library. His cheek twitched and he pulled his coat collar high up around his neck.

March, and I sat on a stool looking out the window of the Chock Full O'Nuts at 116th Street and Broadway, watching the subway entrance. The sun burned through the plate glass, and the four cups of coffee I had already drunk were making me so hot that the subway entrance seemed to swim. I ordered an orange drink.

April. James started down the steps of the New York Public Library. Forty-second Street was jammed with marchers. It was a peace demonstration and they were walking – carrying signs, carrying babies – to the U.N. Some were singing. On the other side of

Fifth Avenue, a girl in dark glasses and a trenchcoat jumped up and down, apparently waving to him. He ducked his head and slipped in among the New Jersey contingent, whose signs proclaimed that they had walked from New Brunswick. Someone handed him a sign. He held it in front of his face and crossed Fifth Avenue. The girl in dark glasses greeted her friend, a woman in tweeds, and they walked off toward Peck & Peck. I stepped out from behind the south lion and joined the march.

And then May. I was baby-sitting for another faculty wife, who supplied me with an infant in yellow overalls and a large aluminum stroller. Under new leaves, cinematically green, we travelled slowly back and forth, bumping over the bricks of Campus Walk, courting sunstroke. It was my most effective disguise. I concentrated my attention on Hamilton Hall, trying to see in the windows. Suddenly there was a rending howl from the stroller. I went rigid with shock; I had forgotten about the baby. James, disguised as a Ph.D., left by a side entrance.

June. Once again I was in that doorway on Carmine Street. I was always standing in that doorway. I was about to cry, and then I walked down the street unable to stop crying. I didn't know where I was going.

And so I lived in the one room I had sublet all that summer. I can still see it. There was a couch, a grand piano, and a window that looked out onto a tree and the back of Our Lady of Pompeii School. (The first morning, I was abruptly awakened by a loudspeaker ordering me to wear my hat tomorrow, to Mass. I was confused; I didn't think I had a hat.) The couch, the piano, and I were the three largest objects in the apartment, and we felt a kinship. It was very quiet when the school term ended. I slept on the couch and set my orange-juice glasses on the grand piano. The one or two people whom I knew in New York seemed to have left for the summer. They were faculty people anyway – more James' friends than mine. The part-time job I had in a branch of the Public Library was over; they had gone on summer hours.

I see it so clearly – the window, the couch, the glass on the piano. It is as if I am still there and that endless summer is just beginning. I pour a little more gin in my orange juice. I am drinking orange juice because it has Vitamin C, and I don't like gin straight. Gin is for sleep; it is infallible. I sit on the couch facing the piano and switch the light off behind me. Through the leaves of the tree I can see the lighted back windows of Leroy Street. The dark air coming in my open window is sweet, smelling of night, garbage, and cats. Sounds hover just outside, hesitating to cross the sill. I lean to hear them, and sit in the window, placing my orange juice on the fire escape. Down through the black iron slats I can dimly make out one... two, three neighborhood cats stalking each other, brushing through the high weeds, converging toward some lusty surprise. On the top of the piano there is a metronome. I reach over and release its armature. The pendulum swings free – *tock*-over, *tock*-over. I sit looking out across the night. *Tock* in the heavy, slow darkness. *Tock*-over. People framed in the Leroy Street windows are eating at tables, talking soundlessly, passing back and forth. Yellow light filters down in shadows, through the leaves and onto the court, darkly outlining the high wild grass, the rusted cans and gray bottles. I reach over and slide the weight all the way down. The pendulum springs away from my hand, ticking wildly, gathering velocity. Accelerando! In the dark below, the cats dance.

When I awake the next morning, it is already hot and my head hurts. I carefully circle the piano and fill the bathroom basin with cold water. I plunge my face into it, staring down through the cold at the pockmarked porcelain, the gray rubber stopper, until my lungs hurt. After a few minutes, I leave the apartment, bangs dripping, walk through the dark hallway, down a flight of stairs, and out onto the burning pavement of Carmine Street. Pushing against the heat, I cross to the luncheonette on Father Demo Square. This is where I buy my morning ice-cream sandwich. The ice cream is for protein, its cold for my head; the two chocolate-cookie layers merely make it manageable. The sun dries my wet bangs into stiff points over my throbbing forehead. I squint and wish I had my dark glasses. Standing by the corner of Bleecker and Sixth Avenue is a glaring white metal pushcart. A squat man in white pants and rolled shirtsleeves leans a hairy arm on its handle and with the other wipes his brow beneath his white cap. Along the side of the cart, brown letters on a yellow background announce, "Chocolate Malt Good Humor." I walk toward the sign, drawn slowly across Bleecker Street. On the sidewalk chairs at Provenzano's Fish Market two old Italians are slipping clams down their throats, sipping juice from the shells. Dead fish, plumped in barrels of ice, eye me, baleful but cool. The air smells of fish and lemon. I confront the Good Humor man and we squint at each other.

"Chocolate Malt Good Humor," I say.

The next week, the Good Humor flavor changes. As I cross Carmine Street, dry-mouthed and stunned in the sunny morning, I read, "Strawberry Shortcake Good Humor." The letters, red against pink, vibrate in the glare. Behind the Good Humor cart, Bleecker Street is in motion. Provenzano's has strung black-and-silver eels in the window. The shop awnings are unrolled, and the canopied vegetable carts form an arcade up toward Seventh Avenue. Italian housewives in black are arguing with the vendors, ruffling lettuces, squeezing the hot flesh of tomatoes, fondling gross, purple eggplants. Ice melts and runs from the fish barrels. I tear the wrapper off my Good Humor – frozen cake crumbs over strawberry-rippled vanilla ice cream – and, tasting its cold, proceed up this noisy galleria. My sandals leak, and I hold my breath passing the clam bar. Loose cabbage leaves scush under my soles, and strawberry sherbet runs down the stick onto my fingers. It is another hot day. At one o'clock, the Department of Parks outdoor swimming pool on the corner of Carmine, where Seventh Avenue becomes Varick Street, is going to open. I have discovered that for thirty-five cents I can stay there until seven in the evening, swimming endless lengths, pastorally shielded from Seventh Avenue by the bathhouse and the two-story Hudson Park branch Public Library. There my neighbors and I lie and tan on the hot city cement, shivering when the late-afternoon shadow of the building creeps over the pale water and turns it dark green. I stay there late every day, until all warmth is gone and evening falls. I no longer cry. I merely wait.

In the last week of June (Coconut Good Humor – a shaggy, all-white confection of shredded coconut frozen on vanilla ice cream), I receive a letter from a Fifth Avenue lawyer telling me that he represents James and that I must consult him in his offices. I find his address formidable. It reminds me that I have not left my safe, low neighborhood for weeks. When I arrive, the lawyer is all smiles and amiability. I sit tensely, feeling strange in white gloves and high heels, while he tells me that James is in Reno, establishing a residence. He asks me if I have a lawyer of my own. I shake my head; I do not want a lawyer. This seems to surprise and annoy him. He shows me a paper that I may sign delegating some Nevada lawyer to represent me. It is only a form, but it is necessary. When it is all over, he says I may have some money, a fair and equable share of our joint assets – if I sign the paper. He offers me a cigarette while I think about it, but I am wearing gloves and I refuse. I do not want to take them off, as if this gesture will somehow make me vulnerable. My gloved hands in my lap look strange, too white below my brown arms. I stare at them and wish I were back on Carmine Street. The lawyer's office is very elegant, with green velvet curtains and an Oriental rug. There is a slim-legged sofa and a low, marble-topped coffee table. All of the walls are panelled in dark oak, and there is a fireplace. I wonder who he is trying to kid. The lawyer pretends to reasonableness. I only want to see James. I do not want to sign anything. I shake my head; I will wait. He looks pained. He does not say so, but he manages to indicate that I am being foolish and unreasonable. I nod yes, and sit mutely. I want to tell this man that when James comes home I am going to be perfect. I wish someone could tell James now that I have stopped crying. The lawyer sighs and takes out a summons, explaining that he is serving me now, if that is all right with me, because he would only have to send someone to serve me with it later. This is saving us both trouble. I nod and hold my hands in my lap. I wonder what would happen if I suddenly jumped up and hid behind the sofa. He extends the paper over his desk, and I watch it come nearer, until it wavers in front of my chest. I reach out and take it. The summons orders me to answer James' complaint in Nevada within twenty days and give reason why I should not be divorced, or be judged by default. I fold the summons in half and put it in my straw handbag. The lawyer smiles, still talking as he walks me to the elevator and shakes my hand. I am glad I am wearing gloves. He is not my friend.

On the Fourth of July, the Good Humor company exceeds itself and, in a burst of confectionery patriotism, produces Yankee Doodle Dandy Good Humor. I admire it as I turn it around on its stick.

Frozen red, white, and blue coconut on a thin coating of white encasing strawberry-striped vanilla ice cream. I salute the Good Humor man as he hands me my change.

I spend most of my time at the pool now. On hot days, the whole neighborhood lines Seventh Avenue, waiting to get in. We stand outside the brick bathhouse in the sun, smelling chlorine on the city air and eating ice cream to keep cool – children, housewives with babies, retired men, office workers taking their vacations at home. Inside the bathhouse – women's locker room to the left, men's to the right – we hurry into our bathing suits, stuffing our clothes into green metal lockers. The air is steamy from the showers. Children shriek and splash, running through the icy footbath that leads to the pool. Out in the sunlight, we greet the water with shouts, embracing the cold shock, opening our eyes beneath the silent green chill to see distorted legs of swimmers and then breaking the sun-glazed surface again, into the noise and splashing. I wear my old black racing suit from college and slather white cream over my nose. Around the pool edge, four teen-age lifeguards in orange Department of Parks suits rove the cement or take turns sitting astride the high, painted iron guard chair. They are neighborhood heroes and accept admiration from small boys with rough graciousness. The pool cop rolls up his blue shirtsleeves and sits with his cap off in the doorway of the First Aid Room, drinking Coca-Cola. We greet each other and exchange views on the heat. He looks wistfully at the pale-aqua water, but he is on duty. I line up behind the crowd at the diving board. I am working on my one-and-a-half this week, pounding the yellow plank, trying to get some spring out of the stiff wood. My form is good, and the board conceals what I lack in daring. Sometimes Ray Palumbo, Paul Anthony, and Rocky (I never did learn his last name), three of the guards, practice with me. We criticize each other and take turns holding a bamboo pole out in front of the board, high above the water, for the others to try to dive over and enter the water neatly. I am teaching Ray's little sister, Ellen, to back-dive, and her shoulders are rosy from forgetting to arch. We all stand around the board, dripping in the sun, and talk about swimming. The boys are shy with me and respectful of my age, but with their friends they are great wits; they patrol the pool, chests out for the benefit of the teen-age girls, swinging their whistles before them like censers.

I have begun to know the other regular swimmers, too. Only the very young and the very old are as free as I am. There is Paul's grandfather, who is retired; he swims a stately breaststroke the length of the pool, smiling, with his white head held high. And Mama Vincenzio, a dignified sixty, who arrives each evening resplendent in a black dressmaker suit three feet wide. She waits her turn with us at the four-foot board, wobbles to its end, and drops off, *ka-plunk*. She does this over and over, never sinking more than a foot or two below the surface before she bobs up again: *pasta*. I am not sure that she can swim, but, on the other hand, she doesn't sink, and she propels herself to the ladder as if she were sweeping floors. We smile shyly at each other for two weeks. When I finally ask her why she comes so late, she tells me she cooks supper for ten people each evening. I also recognize Mr. Provenzano, who closes the store at four-thirty in the summer and comes swimming. I have taught him to scull feet first, and now when I pass his store in the mornings he offers me a peeled shrimp or – I hold my breath and swallow – a raw clam. I sit in the sun, dangling my feet in the water, and think of James. I try imagining him around a roulette wheel or on a dude ranch, but it doesn't work. My idea of Reno is limited. I know he should be studying, and I am sure there can't be a good library there. I wonder what he is doing, but I cannot visualize a thing. When I try, his face begins to look like a photograph I have of him, but I know he never looked like that photograph. This frightens me, so I don't think at all. I swim, and in the evenings I drink.

The thirty-first of July is my birthday. It is also the day of our trial. I will not know this, however, until the twenty-seventh of August, when the divorce decree arrives in the mail. In this morning's mail I receive a funny card from my mother and one from my aunts. My mother encloses a small check "to buy something you need." I buy a bottle of Gordon's gin. When I announce my birthday to the Good Humor man, he presents me with a Hawaiian Pineapple Good Humor, gratis. It looks like a good day.

My regular friends are already at the pool when I arrive, and we wave to each other. From the two-foot board, Ellen Palumbo shouts for me to watch. She has lost her rubber band, and long black hair streams over her shoulders. Still waving, she turns carefully backward, balancing on her toes, and then, arching perfectly, as I have taught her, falls *splat* on her shoulders in the water. I wince and smile encouragingly as she surfaces. Rocky is in the water doing laps of flutter kick, holding on to a red Styrofoam kickboard. I get another board from the First Aid Room and join him. We race through the green water, maneuvering around small boys playing water tag; our feet churn spray. Suddenly my shoulder is grabbed and I am ducked from behind by Rocky's ten-year-old brother, Tony. My kickboard bobs away, and Rocky and I go after Tony, who is swimming quickly to the deep end. He escapes up the ladder and races to the diving board. Thumbing his nose, he executes a comic dive in jackknife position, one leg extended, ending in a high, satisfying splash. It is the signal for follow-the-leader. With shouts, children arrive from all sides of the pool, throwing themselves off the yellow board in imitation.

On the deck, Paul's grandfather is sunning himself, eyes closed, smiling upward toward heaven. I pull myself out of the water and join him. He squints and grins toothlessly, delighted to have someone to talk to. The night before, he has been to see a free, outdoor Shakespeare performance. A mobile theatre unit is performing in our neighborhood this week, in Walker Park Playground. We sit together in puddles on the cement, leaning against the hot bathhouse wall, and he tells me the story of "King Lear." He has been going to the free Shakespeare performances every summer since they began and has seen each play two or three times, except for "Richard II;" he saw that one six times. We watch the boys diving, and he proudly lists all the plays he has seen. When I admit that I have never seen one of the open-air performances, he says I must. He thinks for a minute, then shyly offers to escort me. He will wait in the ticket line at Walker Park this evening and save me a place. I protest, but he says he has nothing at all to do in the evening and he probably will go again. I tell him it is my birthday. He smiles; July is a good month to be born. See? – he holds up his wrinkled, brown hands and turns them over in the sun; on the second of July he was seventy.

When I arrive at the playground that evening, the line seems endless. It stretches along Hudson Street, and I pass whole families seated on the cement, eating supper out of paper bags, reading books, playing cards. Ice cream vendors wheel carts up and down. I recognize my Good Humor man, and we wave to each other. He is selling sherbet sticks to two girls. Frost steams up from the cold depths when he opens his cart. Mr. Anthony is at the front of the line; he must have been waiting for hours. He is wearing a good black wool suit, of an old-fashioned cut. It is a little too big, as if he has shrunk within it. I suspect that it is the suit he wears to weddings and funerals, and I am glad that I have put on my green linen dress, even if it will go limp in the heat.

I have braided my wet hair and wound it round my head in a damp coronet. I look like a lady. We smile shyly, proud of our finery.

At eight, the line begins moving into the playground, where the Parks Department has put up wooden bleachers. They form a semi-circle around the mobile stage; folding chairs are ranged in rows in front of the bleachers. We surge through the entrance with the crowd and find seats quite close to the apron. Behind the gray scaffolding of the stage I can see the wall of the handball court and the trees on Leroy Street; to the south, the old Food and Maritime Trades High School. Trumpets and recorded Elizabethan music herald our arrival. The crowd fills the playground, and the sky gradually darkens. Floodlights dim, and light falls upon the scaffolding. Onstage, Lear summons his three daughters; the play begins. Mr. Anthony and I lean forward from our folding chairs, drawn into the court of Britain. Under the calm, blinking stars, Lear runs mad, contending with the far-off rumble of traffic on Hudson Street. High above, an airplane passes.

During intermission, I tell Mr. Anthony all I can remember about the Elizabethan stage, of the theatre that was a wooden O. We eat ice cream out of Dixie cups with miniature wooden paddles, and he compliments me. I would be a good teacher; in this city they need teachers. Later, as the final act closes, we sit and weep, on our folding chairs, for Lear, for Cordelia, for ourselves. "Never, never, never, never, never." Floodlights open over the playground; it is over. We crowd out with a thousand others on to Clarkson Street, past the dark swimming pool that is reflecting the street lights, to Seventh Avenue. On the way home, Mr. Anthony buys me a glass of red wine at Emilio's to celebrate. We walk by the dark steps of Our Lady of Pompeii, and on my doorstep we smile at each other and shake hands.

On August 27th, the decree arrives – four pieces of typed paper stapled to heavy blue backing, with two gold seals. It looks like a diploma. I read it in the doorway, then walk back upstairs and drop it inside the lid of the grand piano. It is all over, but just now I am late. I eat my Toasted Almond Good Humor hurriedly, on my way to the pool. The Parks Department has been giving free swimming lessons to beginners, from ten o'clock to twelve o'clock in the mornings, and I help teach. When I get there, there are at least thirty children waiting for me around the pool edge, kicking their feet in the water.

That summer, Labor Day Weekend comes early. Few people in my neighborhood are leaving town, and the pool is crowded; everyone goes swimming. The pool will be closing soon. It is my last swim. Tomorrow I begin at P.S. 84 as a substitute teacher; I want to find out if Mr. Anthony is right. The day is hot, making the water icy by contrast. My bathing suit has bleached to a sooty gray now, and my wet hair drips in a long braid down my back. Children shout and splash, and the tarred seams on the pool bottom leap and break in refracted patterns on the moving water. At the far end, in the playground, old men throw boccie. My dark glasses begin sliding down the white cream on my nose. I push them up and join my friends sunning beyond the diving boards. The Good Humor man has parked his truck in the street, just beyond the wire fence. Children range the fence, handing dimes and nickels through, carefully drawing ice-cream sticks in. Mama Vincenzio has come early today, and she buys this week's special, Seven Layer Cake Super Humor, for her two noisy grandchildren and me. We eat them carefully, backs to the sun, counting to make sure we get seven different layers of ice cream and alternating chocolate. The children's faces smear with melted chocolate, and ice cream runs down my arm to the elbow. I toss my stick in the trashcan and dive into the water. The green chill slides over me, and I move in long strokes toward the bottom, cool and weightless. Ellen Palumbo passes me and we bubble faces at each other. When my air runs out, I pick up a stray bobby pin as my civic duty (it would leave a rust mark on the bottom) and, flexing, push to the surface. Oooh.

From the guard chair, Ray beckons to me, and I swim over. For weeks, Rocky and Ray have been working on flips, somersaulting in tucked position. They have reached a point where they have perfected a double flip – two of them, arms linked, somersaulting in unison. All of the younger boys have been imitating them, working variations – forward, backward, spinning in twos above the green water. We have had one broken leg. Now Ray thinks that a triple flip can be done. No one has tried it yet, but if they can do a double – why not? It will be dangerous, of course. If anyone is off, everyone may get hurt. You have to have reliable buddies. He and Rocky wonder if I will try it with them. I'm not as daring as their friends, but my form is better. I won't open at the wrong time. They tell me that I always keep my head. I swallow, standing there in the sun, and wonder if they have ever seen me weeping up a fit over on the Gansevoort Pier, crying into the Hudson as I angrily skip stones. I nod and promise not to crack us up. I am apprehensive.

Rocky grins and chases everyone off the board. Children stand around, dripping puddles, watching us as we carefully pace to the end. The sun burns our shoulders, and the board wavers and dips as our combined weight passes the fulcrum. Above, the sky is bright blue. We link upper arms tightly to make a pivot of our shoulders, and at Rocky's signal we begin flexing for spring, playing the board. "Now!" We are lifted and thrown upward, tucking into the air. The pool turns upside down, sky spins over our knees, the bathhouse revolves. We turn, holding together like monkeys, high above the glazed water. I have a snapshot Mr. Provenzano took of that historic moment. In it, we hang, crouched against the sky, backsides to heaven; one second later we will cut the water together, perfectly straight, to shouts and cheering. We break apart underwater and surface separately, mouths open, to the applause of our small pupils, who rim the deep end and now flop into the water like seals. On the deck, we congratulate each other, shaking hands. Then Rocky climbs the playground wall and high dives, just missing the cement, into the deep end. It is the traditional signal to close the pool. He surfaces, puts on his orange Department of Parks poncho, and the guards begin blowing their whistles; everybody out of the pool. Summer is over.

When I leave the bathhouse, the sun is slanting. Walking up Carmine Street, I buy myself a Chocolate Eclair Good Humor as a reward. The long summer is over at last. Summer is over, and I have kept my head.

The next summer was different.

WAPAKONETA

WHEN THE BALTIMORE & OHIO stopped in Wapakoneta, Anne Martin was the only passenger to get off. The train pulled away, diminishing rapidly down the weed-fringed track, leaving her stunned and blinking in the July sun. She stood alone on the gravel siding. The backs of her knees still smarted from the hot plush seat and her suitcase lay slanted on its side where the conductor had dropped it down to her. They don't waste much time over Wapakoneta, she thought.

The noon sun beat straight down; the sky was blue and cloudless. Anne reached for her dark glasses, balanced above her forehead, and slid them forward onto her nose – the brown-glass tinted waves of heat and dust were still rising from the deserted track. Hitching her suitcase, she walked down the gravel siding toward the station house, crossing a patch of burnt grass. The door of the waiting room stood open, but the ticket window was shuttered and there was no station master in sight. Beyond the station, the ground sloped away to a sparsely graveled parking area and the back entrances of one- and two-story buildings. Anne started down the grade, dragging her suitcase through the weeds and Queen Anne's lace. Three cars were parked at angles, their metal hoods baking in the sun. She passed them, feeling gravel sift under her sandals. Running along the buildings was a dirt alleyway banked by high grass and parked delivery trucks. Further on, the river curved and she could see the gray metal trapezoid of the bridge rising above the trees.

There's the Auglaize River, she thought, at least I know where I am. I'll end up at the bridge. She walked down the alley looking at the rear entrances of stores, trying to remember the town as she'd last seen it. Woolworth's, Penney's, Western Auto. She'd spent her childhood summers here. Milk cans glaring in the sun were stacked shoulder-high against the back wall of the dairy and a sour, cheesy smell wafted through the screen door. We used to come here to get ice cream, she remembered, resting her suitcase in the dust, watching the flies buzz around the screen. I could go in and telephone but I'm almost home now. Once I get to the bridge, it's only a few blocks.

She had told the aunts not to meet her. Fredonia still worked as a secretary in the local machine-tool factory, although they must have known she was three years past retirement age; she had worked there since she was twenty. And Alma Rose, who had retired and might have met her, was recovering from a cataract operation. Neither aunt had ever married and they still lived in the house where they had been born. "I've sublet my New York apartment for two months," she told them when she called from Akron the evening before, "and I need a quiet place to stay for a while and finish some work."

Over the phone she heard Fredonia saying to Alma in the background, "It's Emma Anne in Akron." Then loudly, "Emma Anne, how's your mom and dad up there? We haven't had a letter for a month." Her father was the aunts' younger brother. "This certainly is a surprise for us, Emma Anne. Rose and I were just playing Scrabble and I said, I wonder who could be calling us at this hour." It had been nine-thirty.

"Look, Aunt Doe," Anne had said, "I won't be any trouble. All I want is a place to rest and work on my thesis. I could set a card table up in the front parlor and not bother anybody. There isn't room for me at home, not since they moved to the apartment. Anyhow, I thought it might be nice to be in a house again."

Anne lifted her suitcase, scattering pebbles, and continued past the dairy toward the river. At the end of the street was the haberdashery that her grandfather once held a half interest in. He had died long before she was born, but the store was still called Reade & Foltz when she was a child. Somewhere there was a photograph of her grandfather and Mr. Foltz behind the counter. Had her grandfather had a mustache? I've got to get Alma to show me the albums, she decided. I'm coming home. It's been a long time.

She was approaching the river now and could see the yellow water of the Auglaize moving slowly past its flowering bank. Insects buzzed under the hot weeds at the water's edge and the fume of the river lifted suddenly in a sluggish wave, hitting her nostrils like a slap. Anne stopped, resting her suitcase in the weeds. The rich spoiled smell of the river rose on the sun all around her. Further along the bank, tall trees cast shadows on the water. The last time she had seen that river, she'd been a child, hair flying as she dashed through the high slicing weeds, an angry tomboy pursued by her own fear of growing up. She had been eleven that summer. The summer she fell out of the pear tree. I'm old enough to have a child of my own, she thought, looking at the water. I wonder why it's so yellow? It was always such a yellow river.

When she turned up Elm Street, the house was on the corner, white and square, looking no different. Anne carried her suitcase over the lawn and up the back porch steps. There were five doors into the house, but everyone always entered through the kitchen. Anne peered through the screen door: "Aunt Alma?" She opened the door, feeling the screen sag, and let it bang loudly behind her. Anne stood in the kitchen looking about; the wooden cabinets had been painted white but the lead-topped sink still stood beside the stove. The kitchen smelled faintly of flour, as it always had. Anne crossed to the cabinet and pulled out the slanting wooden flour bin. The flour was still kept there, but now it lay sealed in a commercial package. She remembered her grandmother standing in front of the stove, framed in light from the window, reaching over to pick out a handful of flour for gravy. She let the bin rock back into place, hesitating to open the other drawers. As children her cousins and she had always gone straight to the string drawer on their arrival to see if their "treasure" was intact. There should have been a biscuit tin with metal jackstones – forty-two of them, she remembered – a tin kazoo, and her grandfather's silver badge from the Wapakoneta Volunteer Fire Department.

Dear God, she thought, I haven't seen any of them for years. They were always there. I don't want to know. The door to the pantry was standing open and she crossed to it.

Inside the pantry the trapdoor was pulled up, leaving a gaping square through the floor. Alma must have gone down to the cellar. Anne approached the opening cautiously and looked down. The trapdoor had always been dangerous. Her grandmother had forgotten it was open and stepped over the edge when she was eighty-seven and still doing the cooking. She had lain at the bottom with a broken hip for two hours until the aunts had come home from work, and although she died at ninety-two, she had never been quite as active again. They'll probably both go like that, Anne worried, looking down. "Alma, Aunt Alma?"

Along three walls of the pantry were shelves stacked with tins and preserves, quart mason jars with homemade pickles and short wax-topped glasses of apple jelly. Anne stared at a blue sugar canister with a dented lid. That's older than I am. It had always been filled with homemade cookies, thin ones with floury edges cut out of dough with an upturned water glass. She reached out to open the tin.

"Emma Anne," her aunt's face appeared, a white circle in the dark below. "Why, I didn't hear anyone come in." The face grew in circumference beneath Anne's feet as Alma progressed up the steep stairs. Light glinted off the thick rimless glasses Alma had always worn. Her aunt's body heaved upward step by step through the floor, reaching Anne's knees.

"Hello, Aunt Alma," Anne said, prying the tin open. It was full of Oreos.

St. Theresa: The Little Flower, Men of Maryknoll, Damian the Leper, The Keys of the Kingdom, Our Lady of Fatima... Anne was looking through the glass door of the sitting room bookcase after supper. She remembered them all; she had read each one several times as a child. Fredonia was outside hanging dishtowels on the line, having carefully spilled dishwater over the peonies to discourage ants. Alma moved about setting up the card table for fan-tan.

"Aunt Alma," Anne said turning, "have you kept up the scrap-books?"

Her aunt set the cigar box of pennies that they used for poker chips on the table and began counting them into piles. She looked up through her heavy lenses. "Well, I've saved everything, but I haven't pasted any of it for years. I meant to do it when I retired, but my eyes aren't what they used to be." She sighed.

"Can I take a look tonight?" Anne asked, turning the key in the glass bookcase door.

"What in heaven's name can you want in that bookcase, Emma Anne?"

"Oh," Anne turned the key back. "Nothing, I guess. Just habit. We used to open everything, didn't we? Do you remember the time Mary Lou and I locked Evaleen in the little attic under the eaves?" Anne laughed. "Remember when Doe caught us prying the lid off the cistern?"

"Little Evaleen," Alma said. "You and Mary Lou were so mean to that poor child."

"She was a tattletale," Anne said firmly, "and a drag. Those Shirley Temple curls."

"You were both jealous."

"Weren't we, though? Everyone made such a fuss over Ev because she was the youngest. I had pigtails and Mary Lou looked like a blimp. We would have cut those curls off, but Lou was always afraid of Aunt Bridget. Little Evaleen," Anne mused. "You know we tried to set her on fire once."

"Emma Anne!"

"Well, we didn't *succeed*." Anne sat at the card table. "I really liked Ev the last time I saw her – at Lou's wedding. Anyway, Lou turned out to be the family beauty. Ev's hair went straight later. Have you seen them lately?"

"I remember whenever you and Mary Lou wanted anything you used to make Little Evaleen do the asking."

"She had her uses," Anne smiled.

Alma continued. "Mary Lou and Jack were down over Easter with Mark, Patty, and Little Mike. Mary Lou's expecting again in November."

"Has she got three now?" Anne asked. "We never had much in common after we stopped coming here in the summer. I haven't seen them since I moved to New York."

"You ought to live at home with your mother and dad," Alma said. "They worry about you. Doe and I were so happy to hear that you finally decided to come home."

"Only for the summer," Anne interrupted quickly. "I just got tired of the crowds, and I hadn't been to Akron since they sold the house."

"Five years," her aunt said putting her lips together. "I think it's a disgrace, Emma Anne, the way you choose to live all alone so far from your family."

"Aunt Alma," Anne protested. "They have their own lives. I'm grown up. Anyway there isn't room for me now. Alma, I've lived in New York for the last five years. Ohio isn't my home anymore."

"Your home is where your family is… "

Fredonia appeared in the doorway. "What's this Emma Anne is saying?" She came in slowly, carrying three saucers of ice cream with chocolate sauce, and set them on the card table. "I thought we might like to have a 'dope' before we get started."

Anne smiled at the familiar Wapakoneta term. "I'm not sure I remember how to play." She spooned into the melting ice cream, watching chocolate syrup fill the indentation. The aunts' spoons clicked in their saucers.

The clock above the bookcase ticked through the pause.

Anne looked up uncomfortably. "The house does seem quiet, though. There were always so many of us those summers. I've never been to Wapak when Grandma Reade wasn't here."

"She had a very happy death," Doe said, "and the last sacraments only two days before the end. The six o'clock mass tomorrow is our mass – a memorial mass for Mom – although we generally do go to the seven. We get a ride home with the Farrs."

Anne had not come home for her grandmother's funeral. She had told her parents that she couldn't come; that her presence at the graveside would do her grandmother no good anyway. She hated family burials, which inevitably ended in a great spread of food laid on for the out-of-town mourners. The truth was, she supposed, that she'd been afraid. She might have had to explain her life. Someone might have asked her where James was. She should have gone though, simply to spare her parents embarrassment. Anne hadn't been to church for five years. The aunts went to mass daily – as did her parents, and as she had all through her childhood. Anne looked up, realizing that Alma was talking.

". . . remarkable the way she kept all her faculties right up to the very end. Mom always said she intended to die at home; and she breathed her last right upstairs in her own bed." Alma fanned herself with a folded newspaper from the chair. "That last week, when the doctor said she might go any day, Doe and I took turns staying home from work to look after her. But Mom waited and died on the Saturday – so we were both with her to the last. And don't you know, at the very end, I swear she looked straight up, past us, as if she were seeing something there that we couldn't see... "

Doe broke in quickly, "They say that at the hour of death, if you die in a state of grace, God lets you see your guardian angel."

Anne looked at her aunts, who were both fanning themselves in the silent room, and felt suddenly very hot and defeated. "Yes," she nodded. "Yes, I've heard that you can."

Anne carried the scrapbook into her grandmother's bedroom and dropped it in the middle of the bed. The upstairs was hot and the air hung in layers with a dry, brown-wood smell from the eaves.

Both screened windows were open but no air stirred. She switched off the hanging light bulb and dragged the bedside table lamp closer. On the wall opposite, a picture of the Sacred Heart looked down from a wide black frame. One of its hands pointed accusingly to the thorn-wreathed heart flaming out of its breast; the other was raised in benediction over her head. As a child she'd been terrified of that picture. Now she turned to meet its baleful stare and raised her hand, returning the blessing, then she looked about. Her grandmother's bed had a high headboard flush with the ceiling and there was a marble-topped washstand lined with framed snapshots of grandchildren. In front of these lay a hairbrush and her grandmother's black rosary, neatly coiled.

Anne crawled up onto the big bed, feeling the mattress sag, and opened the bulging scrapbook. Alma's scrapbook was a family history – one her aunt had begun thirty years ago – of family papers, photographs, and snapshots, embellished with captions in colored type Alma had cut from magazines. It was nearly five inches thick now and loose papers trailed from its pages. As children, Anne and her cousins had begged to look through it. She opened to the middle where her generation began to see if anything new had been added and smiled at the familiar baby photos. Above hers Alma had pasted a blue butterfly and the words OUR EMMA ANNE. Mary Lou had gotten a frame of gold stars. She turned the pages looking at snapshots: Lou staring out of her baby carriage. Anne in a Dutch bob pedaling a tricycle. Ev's birth. The three of them one summer, lined on the porch steps, squinting into the sun. Anne tried to remember a smaller size of her own flesh. How had it felt? But the years had passed forever, stopped briefly by the chance of someone taking a snapshot.

Ev in her first communion veil, programs from Lou's piano recitals, Anne a frowning Camp Fire Girl. Lou growing slim. Ev beginning to look nervous. HIGH SCHOOL GRADUATION. Her scholarship announcement and Lou's engagement photo. A single picture postcard of her college, then five pages: WEDDING BELLS, OUR MARY LOU AND JACK. Formal bridal photos, pressed white roses, snapshots – all the relatives eating cake. Anne turned the page: a series of baby pictures began, Lou's three. She flipped past Lou's most recent child and her own wedding stared back at her. James looking terribly young in his dark suit. Anne wearing her favorite green linen dress, holding an elaborate bouquet her mother had ordered despite Anne's objections. Like the record of *Lohengrin* her mother had put on the phonograph when they returned to the house. Small snapshots, all taken by her father. She and James were in graduate school and determined to spend little time or money on ceremony. The two of them grinned out of the snapshot, laughing at the fancy bouquet. "You fools," she told the photograph. Anne and James drinking scotch in the living room with Father O'Connell. They had finally married at St. Francis to please her parents, but in the rectory. Anne and James in raincoats, setting off to drive back to New York, mugging at the camera through the rain, water dripping off their hair. Anne waving – you could see her wedding ring. They hadn't ever told anyone it came from Woolworth's. That had been their joke; the very same ring that they'd used during the school year to check into hotels. The only real bit of sentiment in the whole ceremony.

"Nice try," she said grimly and let the scrapbook fall closed. The hot air hung heavy in the room; the bed creaked and sagged. Anne set the scrapbook on a nearby chair and switched off the light. From the window she could see the still, black leaves of the trees. There were fireflies in the garden below.

It was dark when they set off for mass. The sun had begun rising, drying the damp pavement as they walked. Crossing Wapakoneta Bridge, Anne watched the sun move down the surface of the water, yellowing the silt that flowed slowly above the deeper green. Bank grass, bowed with dew, leaned darkened points into the water. All around her, she could feel heat rising to dry the day. The sun's early burning rays slanted a long way toward them from the horizon. Standing on the bridge, Alma took out a handkerchief and wiped her brow, predicting that the day "looked like another scorcher."

St. Joseph's Church was dark except for the sanctuary lamp and some flickering votive candles banked before the side altar. Four nuns from the parochial school knelt in the front pew; as the bell tinkled to announce the mass, they rose in consecutive rustles and an old priest emerged from the sacristy. He was wearing black vestments and carried a veiled chalice. Anne stood with her aunts, reaching up to straighten the hat Fredonia had lent her. She'd tried to leave the house without one, but they'd stopped her on the porch, insisting she wear a hat, and pinned one of Doe's on her head, securing it with a long hatpin. The hat was straw, nest-shaped with velvet leaves and wisps of veiling. The hatpin pulled Anne's hair whenever she bowed her head, so she held her chin well up, knowing she looked comic with her long hair, cotton skirt, and sandals.

Incense from past masses floated in the hot recesses of the vaulted ceiling. Anne's nostrils pricked to the heavy liturgical smell. She knelt, watching the priest before the lighted altar, remembering early morning masses at the small convent boarding school she'd attended, mostly masses offered for the dead – dead the students did not know. At six a.m. in the candlelit school chapel they sang the Dies Irae on empty stomachs. Little girls in white chapel veils, watching clouds of incense rise in a yellow haze. "Dies irae, Dies illa, Solvet saeclum in favilla... " She had seen angels in that incense. Very often someone fainted.

They met the Farrs after mass in the church parking lot. Anne didn't know them, but on the walk to church her aunts had talked enthusiastically about the Farrs and their twenty-two-year-old daughter, Helen. They went to mass daily and always gave the aunts a ride home. Helen Farr was joining the novitiate of the Sisters of Mercy in September. All last year she had taught second grade at St. Joseph's school because there was a shortage of nuns. Alma had gone on much too pointedly about Helen Farr for Anne to bear. Helen had graduated from a Catholic college.

"I've never heard of Mercycrest," Anne said flatly. "Is it accredited?"

The Farrs were waiting by their new Buick. Anne bent down into the back seat with her aunts, removing the hat and hairpin. Her scalp felt hot and scratched. Helen Farr was sitting in front between her parents. Helen had short brown hair, freckled skin, and wore a shirt dress. I may be three years older than she is, Anne thought, but I look younger. She smiled at Helen Farr.

Mrs. Farr turned and addressed Anne. "It's so nice to finally meet you, Emma Anne, dear. Your aunts have told us so much about you. You're a teacher, aren't you?"

"No," she said, "I'm finishing a graduate degree at Columbia, in English literature. This summer I'm revising my thesis to submit in the fall."

Mrs. Farr looked confused. "Well, anyway," she went on, "your nice aunts here have told us so much about you and your clever professor husband."

Anne looked up sharply and caught sight of Doe's face and Alma looking worried. Oh, my God, she thought, they haven't told anyone

I'm divorced. I've been divorced for two years and they can't admit it. The shame is too great.

"James is in New York," she said quickly. "He had to teach a summer school course – one of the men in the department got sick – so I came by myself." She looked around. Everyone seemed to accept that.

After breakfast, Anne carried the portable typewriter out onto the front porch and set it on the card table. The porch stretched in shadow across the house and around one side. Honeysuckle and thick-leaved vines twined over the railing to the roof. It was already too hot. Anne sat on the slatted porch swing and kicked off her sandals. The chains creaked slowly. She lifted her heavy hair to cool her neck. The metal thermometer by the door read ninety-two degrees. Through the screened window she could see Alma bent over the ironing board, alternately ironing and fanning herself, and she remembered her grandmother doing the same thing. "Aunt Alma," Anne called, "is that swimming pool by the playground – the one we always went to – still open?"

By lunchtime the temperature had risen to ninety-four. Alma carried a plate of egg salad sandwiches and a pitcher of lemonade out onto the porch where Doe, who had walked home on her lunch hour, sat on the swing in her stocking feet, fanning. Her white perforated health shoes lay airing below as she swayed. Anne sat barefoot on the porch steps, leaning against a post. She bit into a limp sandwich, spilling egg salad onto her bare knees, and jiggling ice cubes in her lemonade.

"They say at work that the heat's going to last all week," Doe announced. "It's been bad for the fair this year – people don't want to walk around in all this heat looking at animals. You can imagine the smell."

"Is the county fair on now?" Anne looked up. "We ought to go some night. Remember the summer you took Lou, Ev, and me?" Anne laughed. "The time the Ferris wheel got stuck with Alma and me on top, and they couldn't start it up again."

"You rocked that seat deliberately, Emma Anne," Alma said. "Trying to scare me out of my wits. You always took such risks. Why, we must have stopped up there twenty minutes."

"It was lovely," Anne said. "We could see for miles, the whole fairgrounds. I couldn't have been more than nine. It was my first Ferris wheel." She smiled into her lemonade. "Real Americana. Later Ev's loose tooth came out in the saltwater taffy, and she bled so much you took us all home."

"I don't remember that," Doe said.

"My memory is awfully good lately," Anne admitted. She sucked a wet lemon slice. "I'm beginning to feel about twelve years old again. I suppose that's because nothing has changed here." She drained the last lemonade from the glass. "I think I may just go swimming this afternoon. It's too hot to type."

She walked Doe back to work as far as the bridge, carrying her bathing suit in a rolled towel, then followed the river bank as it wound toward the municipal park and swimming pool. Only a few children were in the playground, swinging in the fierce sunlight. Anne crossed the worn grass, feeling patches of dirt loosen under her bare soles. Waves of heat glared off the metal sliding boards; they looked as if they would blister you at a touch. Beyond a row of swings, the ground sloped upward and Anne could hear the noise of the swimming pool before she saw it. Shouts and splashing; water sounds growing louder. The noon sun burned the edges of her dark glasses. The air smelled of chlorine and hot dogs. Anne pushed the sunglasses higher on the bridge of her sweating nose and started up the prickly grass.

The swimming pool, enclosed by wire playground fencing, was jammed. Children raced between the spread bodies sunning on the deck and flung themselves into the water. Spray arched through the air. As Anne drew level she could see the blue rectangle of water splashing with swimmers – pale at the shallow end shading to deep aqua under the diving boards. Red and white floats, strung beadlike across the moving surface, marked the drop-off. At the deep end children lined up, dripping, behind the diving boards. Along the cement deck groups of teenage girls sprawled on towels, talking and combing their wet hair. Oil glistened on their bare limbs.

As Anne watched, a boy sprang the high board, rising in burning outline against the sky before he jackknifed and cut the water in a bright explosion of drops. With shouts, small boys hurled themselves from both low boards. Water flashed up on either side. She shifted her towel, perspiring, and hurried along the fence to the bathhouse.

Anne stood waiting in the sun beneath the high board. The tanned legs of a diver were disappearing up the ladder. In a few seconds he would be above and gone. Anne gripped the tubing rungs and started up. Overhead the board dipped and vibrated. As his body cut the water, she saw his feet overthrow: too much arch. Clutching the guard rail, Anne pulled herself atop the platform and held tightly. She had always been a little afraid up here. The board was covered in rough cocoa matting and stretched over the water; below, the pool was bright aqua. Children raced and shouted on the deck. The sky overhead was drifting with clouds. Beyond the pool fence she could see swings in the playground and the baseball diamond. Distant fields stretched away to farmland, roads curved through summer weeds toward town. Through the familiar landscape, taking its time, the slow yellow water of the Auglaize River flowed as if it had all summer to reach Lake Erie.

Anne straightened, sucking in her stomach, and carefully paced to a few feet from the end. The sun was hot on her shoulders. I'm going to burn, she thought. The board dipped as her weight crossed the fulcrum. She flexed and began her approach. One, two – on the third step she hurdled, landing to force the plank down. The board dipped and recoiled, throwing her upward into the air. Rising, she saw the clouds move. Anne brought her arms together – the water was rushing toward her eyes.

Down, down through the cold green layers of water, she swam, silent and alone. Far above, sun filtered through the soundless water. She turned deep beneath the surface, arms moving in pale sweeps, and stroked quickly upward following her own air bubbles. Her face broke the sealed surface into the noise and splashing.

Anne shook the wet hair from her eyes and swam a fast crawl to warm up, dodging children, exhaling a cold wake of bubbles that pricked along her arms like ginger ale. Still moving, she swiveled onto her back to rest. The sun was beginning to slant west, marking afternoon.

Anne gave the pool a professional glance; she had spent her college summers lifeguarding at a pool in Akron. There were three guards on duty here. A boy and girl perched on guard chairs while another boy roved the deck, blowing his whistle at small boys who played water tag. The swimmers were mostly kids.

Anne floated, looking up at the sky, remembering Ohio summers full of long days. The sun shone in her face and chlorine stung familiarly in her nostrils. For four summers, she had sat high above the swimmers, water splashing below her tanned legs – watching the afternoon sun cross the Ohio sky and make a sundial of her high, narrow chair. She'd pulled out hundreds of children, but there had never been a drowning or a serious accident. I wouldn't like the responsibility now, she thought. Anyway, I'm out of practice.

Anne sculled, bringing her legs together on the surface. They looked pale against the sun-glazed water. She had learned synchronized swimming in college and swam in the annual water ballet. She tried several ballet legs, one after the other, each toe pointed toward the sky. Not bad. Anne sculled both knees toward her chest, and tried lifting both legs at once. She immediately sank. Coughing, she emerged; she hadn't expected that. She wished she had a nose clip to keep the water out. Determined, Anne shook the wet hair from her eyes and tried a few somersaults, then a kip, extending both legs – toes pointed – as high as she could, before heading toward the bottom. Carried by the momentum of her thrust, Anne plunged straight down through the water. As she descended she saw a child's face, not far away, watching. She plunged deeper and saw another child swimming toward her. Dark braids floated upward as the child came nearer. Anne bubbled and waved. The tinted pool bottom was close now. Anne dropped her legs and, flexing, pushed hard, straight up to the surface. Nearby, the two children emerged. They were both about eleven years old.

"That was… cool… ," the child with the braids gasped, treading water, bobbing up and down with the effort. The second child kicked closer, arms moving in short, splashy strokes. "What was that… will you do it again?" Her hair was cut short with dripping bangs and she was freckled. A nose clip dangled from a peach rubber band around her neck. The questions came in spurts between breaths: "Can't you show us… ?"

Anne motioned them to follow and swam to the side of the pool. Their names were Ginny and Judy, and they came swimming every day.

By five-thirty, the sun's rays stretched along the horizon, casting golden streaks on the water. Anne lay flat on the pool edge, arms and chest extended over the water, holding Ginny's feet as the child tried to arch backward in the water. Anne had somehow acquired two other pupils. They all splashed like a row of frantic seals, while she held their feet.

"If you bend your knees," she warned them, "it's going to look funny."

Judy's nose clip was passed from one child to another. Anne hoped none of them had anything contagious. They looked healthy. She also suspected that some of them should be going home to supper.

Judy climbed onto the deck and sat beside her, panting. "Will you be here tomorrow?" she asked. "Hey." She leaped up, spraying water onto Anne's back. "Ellen."

One of the lifeguards was approaching. She was very young, with cropped curly hair and a deep tan. The sweet, coconut smell of suntan lotion filled the air.

"Hi," the girl said, standing over Anne. "Do you go to college?" Her whistle swung from her hand on a red-and-white lanyard, the kind children braided in camp.

In the water, Ginny gave a desperate sweep with both arms and succeeded in arching under without bending her knees. Anne gave a downward shove on Ginny's ankles to help, then let go. She stood up, rubbing her beveled knees. "Not really," she said. "I've been out of college for years. I'm grown up."

The guard stared at her.

"It's hard to tell when you're wet," Anne said. "And I am in graduate school." Behind them, she heard Ginny scrambling out of the pool.

"Oh." The girl twisted her lanyard around one finger. "I thought you might be – because you do synchronized. I'm going to Ohio State this fall. They have a synchronized program there."

"Her name's Anne, Ellen." Judy came between them. "And she comes from New York City."

"New York," the girl looked at Anne respectfully. "I didn't think you were from Wapakoneta."

Anne put her hands up to shield her eyes from the sun. "I'm visiting my aunts... Reade on Elm Street. I used to spend my summers here when I was small... years ago."

"I'm Ellen Foley," the girl said. "You're very good."

"Not anymore." Anne shook her head. "I'm out of practice." She picked up her towel from the wet deck and wrung it out. Water splashed on the cement.

"We have a swimming group." Ellen let the whistle unwind from her fingers. "In the morning before the pool opens. Bob's sister coaches us. She went to Ohio U. – they have synchronized – but she doesn't know any of the stunts."

"Who's Bob?" Anne asked, draping the wet towel across her sunburned shoulders.

Ellen and Anne began walking toward the bathhouse. Judy and Ginny followed, Judy hopping on one foot to jiggle water out of her ear.

"Judy, you're getting me wet." Ellen gave Anne a look. "*Kids,*" she said. Anne guessed she must be all of eighteen.

"Bob Fuller is the pool manager," she explained. "You probably saw him. He guards sometimes, but mostly he's in the first-aid room, that's the pool office. Bob's at Ohio State now. We date."

Two boys passed them, eating hot dogs. A strong smell of mustard lingered in the air.

"Are you going to be in Wapakoneta long?" Ellen asked.

"A while," Anne said. "I'm trying to type my thesis, but the weather's gotten too hot."

They walked along the deck, trying to place their bare feet on wet patches.

"You could probably teach us a lot," Ellen said. "Sue is coaching the kids to help Bob. He has to put on a water show. We're supposed to have a public demonstration at the end of every summer for the Park Department. You'd like Sue – she's been to New York. She teaches in the junior high school. Sue's taking the show because Bob can't get anyone else. She has little kids at home."

They'd come to the bathhouse; Anne could hear the showers running inside.

Ellen paused, and looked at Anne hopefully. "Would you like to come tomorrow morning and watch?" she asked. "I could introduce you to Sue."

"Please," Judy danced from behind, circling on the hot cement. "Say yes, Anne. You can use my nose clip."

After supper, Anne cleared the table, finishing the remains of the meat loaf in the kitchen, dipping bits of it in catsup with her fingers. She had made lots of meat loaf for James in New York; it was cheap and certain. He called Ohio the Great Midwestern Meat Loaf Belt. Anne smiled, capping the catsup bottle, and piled up the stripped corn cobs. There had been fresh corn on the cob for supper and sliced tomatoes still warm from the afternoon sun. Alma was putting on the kettle to scald the plates. Anne pulled a stiff dish towel off the rack behind the sink. Through the back screen door she could see the sun slanting behind the pear trees. The pears were green and hard looking. It was absolutely still. Anne began drying a water glass.

Doe took a clean towel from the drawer. "You look as if you got some sun today, Emma Anne. You can't be too careful. They say the sun can give you cancer."

"It will tan by tomorrow," Anne said. "By the way, one of the pool guards asked me to stop by tomorrow morning. They need help with their water show. The kids are putting one on in a few weeks and they want me to direct the synchronized swimming. Water ballet," she explained to the aunts. "I think I may just go see what they're doing – if it's this hot again tomorrow."

Alma looked at her.

"One of the guards said she knew you from St. Joseph's," Anne added. "Ellen Foley? The pool manager was young; his name is Bob Fuller."

"Your dad went to school with the Foley boys," Alma said. "Fuller?" She turned to Doe. "Aren't they the ones who used to have the other dry goods store? I don't think they're Catholic," she told Anne.

"Well, I think I will go tomorrow," Anne said. "If only for the practice. I haven't done any serious swimming for years, but it doesn't seem that long." She looked out the screen door. The sun had set and the pear tree flamed.

Doe crossed to the cupboard. "Do you see James up at Columbia?"

"Yes," Anne said. "I see him. He's married again – you knew that, didn't you? He's been married for two years. I don't know her."

"You were married in the church," Alma said. "What God has joined together... "

"James wasn't Catholic. Look, Aunt Alma, the divorce was his idea. I didn't want it. He left me for someone else. For God's sake, Alma, he's been married for two years now and I don't *even know* her."

"You're still married in the eyes of the church," Doe said gently.

"We know how you must feel. I'm surprised that you stay at that school."

"I started a degree at Columbia," Anne said. "I can't transfer now. Anyway I don't want to. Columbia's a huge place, Doe. There are more students going to Columbia than there are people in Wapakoneta."

"That may be, but I don't see that all your education has made you happy." Alma poured kettle water across the dishes. Steam rose from the scalded plates. "Mary Lou never went to college and she seems very happy."

Anne picked up a plate, feeling the hot china burn through the dish towel. "Lou was always happy. When she was little she called all her dolls Patty – so what does she call her firstborn... ?"

"Patty is a good saint's name," Doe said.

"You didn't even play with dolls," Alma reminded Anne. "You were always running wild or reading."

"What you mean is that I haven't any children."

Alma looked up. "I didn't say that." She put the kettle on the stove and crossed the kitchen.

"Alma and I never married," Doe said firmly. "We stayed here to take care of Mom so the boys could marry."

"Didn't you ever want to leave?"

"No," Doe said. "No, we never did. This is our home. We never wanted to leave."

Out in the living room, Anne could see Alma setting up the card table for Scrabble.

Doe turned to her. "You'll always have a home here with us, when you decide, Emma Anne."

Anne squinted behind her dark glasses. The pool deck was dry and the cement glared in the morning sun. She sat on one of the slatted poolside benches, intending only to watch. The swimmers were lined along the pool edge, facing the water. Across the pool a tall young woman in a black bathing suit and wide straw hat was checking names off a clipboard. Her hair was pulled back with a rubber band and her legs looked firm, although her stomach sloped helplessly forward, swelling her suit like a soft ripe fruit as if she'd recently had a child.

Anne counted twenty swimmers, all girls. Some she recognized from the day before. She had slipped in unnoticed, but now Judy spotted her and began waving, poking Ginny. They grabbed each other and teetered on the edge of the pool.

Anne shook her head and frowned. The swimmers shifted restlessly in the heat. They were lined up by height: tall full-chested high-school girls next to long-stalked adolescents. The line descended along the poolside from the mature to the childishly square, ending with the under-twelves, tubby and waistless like hard new buds in their tank suits.

As Anne watched, the instructor moved down the deck and the line straightened. Sunlight reflected off the unbroken blue water, outlining their tanned limbs. The water shimmered, refracting cracks at the bottom. The smell of chlorine was strong and the ten-thirty sun scorched the air like a clean dry iron.

The swimmers tensed forward and the first girl dove; a long shallow dive. The line began to peel off, a ripple of tan bodies, one after the other – striking the water like a breaking wave. Anne could tell they had practiced. The peel was well-timed, although they had trouble emerging in stroke.

"Get those elbows up." The woman in the straw hat was running down the deck beside the lead swimmer. The line of swimmers slanted down the pool, arms splashing, hesitant, carefully watching each other.

"You wouldn't believe they've been doing this for three weeks, would you?" The tall woman was abreast of her, walking backward, watching the swimmers advance. She turned to Anne, "Hello. You must be the one who's come to save us. Bob said he finally got me some help. I'm Sue Chernak."

Anne could see her freckled face under the straw brim. The last two girls dove, finishing the long peel, and the swimmers progressed down the pool, heads high, arms splashing in the sun. The lead swimmer reached the deep end.

"Now they form a circle," Sue said. Anne left the bench, moving beside Sue, following the swimmers. The hot cement burned her soles.

The lead swimmer started to turn, wet ponytail dragging in the water, her long arms churning. The line began to circle: right arm, left arm, closing on itself.

"Jesus," Sue swore as she ran along the pool edge. "Wider, Joanie. Give them more room." She turned to Anne. "Three weeks practice! We're going to use this for the finale. We haven't even tried it to music yet."

The swimmers completed a wide ellipse in the center of the pool and faced inward, treading water.

"Look at that circle." Sue leaned forward. "What are you waiting for? Start the pattern."

Anne watched the swimmers float back. Their tanned legs were refracted and short under the clear water. The legs moved to the surface and broke the water, toes pointed to the center like brown spokes. A shifting kaleidoscope of bright bathing suits and brown arms and legs. Now the legs opened slowly, making wide V's as the pointed toes touched those of swimmers on either side. An enormous uneven star formed on the surface of the water. Some of its shorter points had scabby knees.

Saturday night Anne was invited out for supper. "If you come early," Sue had said over the phone, "we could block out some routines to music before Al gets home. He went to Dayton this morning on business, so he won't be home early. I've told him there's someone in town from New York. He's dying to meet you. Do you drink beer?"

"Yes," Anne had said, "I drink beer." But there are so many people in New York, she'd thought, I'm not special. Still, her small celebrity pleased her. Most of the kids knew her now and said, "Hi," on the street. That afternoon she'd been to the public library. Ellen told her where it was, in the basement of the high-school building. Her aunts had lived in Wapakoneta all their lives and never taken out a library card. Anne registered for one using Alma's name. She had walked home under the old trees carrying her books, feeling safe, looking at large wooden houses and fretted porches. Past lawns. Over walks so old and solid that they had settled into the earth. The pavement ranged up and down. Some of the walks were sunken bricks. I'm tired of New York, she thought. No one cares in New York.

When she got home from the library, Alma was in the kitchen.

"There's lemonade in the ice box, Emma Anne." Alma had looked at the new library card. "We've never been readers," she said. "We have all the books we need."

Sue lived in a yellow, two-story house, wooden and narrow with gray painted floorboards on the front porch. It was not new; the trees that lined the street were enormous. All the houses in Wapakoneta have porches, Anne thought. She looked in through the screen door. The room was filled with furniture-store furniture, new, darkly upholstered, square and anonymous. A wooden playpen filled with toys stood on one side of the room. The rest of the furniture faced the television set, as if the large stuffed pieces were watching the screen.

Sue's probably putting the kids to bed, Anne thought. She rang the bell.

"These glasses were a wedding present," Sue said. She emptied a can of beer into the stemmed goblet that Anne held awkwardly. "Al hates them – they were from my mother – so they only come out for company."

In the background, the record player throbbed: *Tonight, To... night.* Anne was feeling pleasantly drunk. Outside, beyond the porch, the sun was going down pinkly through the trees.

"Al doesn't get along with my mother," Sue explained. "She owns this place. You see, we were living in Dayton when Christopher was born. I had to quit teaching and Al's job didn't pay enough." Sue took a swallow of beer. "Al's always been a salesman – he's in storm doors right now. Well, my family offered to give us this house. Al didn't want to come here; he's from Dayton. I met him at a dance my second year teaching. I lived at the Y.W. – that's where the dance was."

"It's a nice house." Anne lifted her glass and looked through the cold yellow beer out beyond the screen door. "You have an enormous yard."

"Al didn't go to college," Sue said. "My family didn't like the idea of our getting married."

"I was married," Anne said, watching the sun go down behind the trees. "But I've been divorced for two years now. My aunts don't like to admit that. James teaches at Columbia." The sky was darkening

116

and fireflies began to light in the bushes. "It's very peaceful here."

"Al hates it here," Sue replied. "There nothing to do in Wapakoneta. You have to drive to Lima just to see a movie. And then it's never anything you'd want to see." The music switched to "Maria."

"Wapak seems a good place to raise kids," Anne said. "You have two, don't you? James and I didn't have any. Well, I miscarried once, but I don't think that counts. My cousins and I used to love Wapak when we were little."

"Well, I like living in a house," Sue said. "I grew up in a house. You don't get that in New York. I stayed in New York one summer, between teaching jobs – with three other girls. I slept on their couch. It was on West Eighty-eighth Street." She picked up a bowl of potato chips and held it out to Anne. "I liked the advantages of New York – the theater and everything – but it was terribly crowded and hot. There were a lot of Puerto Ricans on our street." Sue took a cigarette and offered the pack. "These kids want to do *West Side Story* for their water show, and they've never even seen a Puerto Rican."

Anne smiled. "But the music is awfully good. For that matter I don't suppose these kids have known many blacks. I don't remember ever seeing blacks in Wapak. Are any living here now?"

"No," Sue said, "but I shouldn't think they'd want to. Too few jobs. In Dayton half my classes were colored." Sue inhaled; white smoke rose from her cigarette in the dusk. "There's not enough work in Wapak to keep our own kids in town – especially if they've gone away to college. I guess we need some light." She got up and switched on a floor lamp. The sudden light made Anne blink. She had been feeling safe in the dusk.

"I taught school for a while," Anne said. "In New York, but only as a substitute. That was before I decided to finish my degree. I could teach, but the kids ran all over me. Subbing's tough."

"Teaching's easier here," Sue said. "I know everybody. The family still counts here. Discipline's not as hard." She picked up a tablet of white paper lying beside the phonograph. "Look, I've got half of 'I Feel Pretty' blocked out for the Juniors. The high-school girls need more work on 'Maria,' and now they want to do 'America,' too."

"'America'? That's awfully fast."

Sue blew smoke out of the side of her mouth. "They insisted. They want to plan their own swimming routines – but they spend most of the time planning their costumes. I'm going to have to step in soon."

She lifted the arm of the phonograph and moved it forward. *Make of our hearts, one heart...* "This is the make-believe wedding. I promised the younger kids that they could do the wedding."

Anne listened. "At least it's slow." She stood and tried several arm strokes in the air. "It ought to be a waltz-crawl."

"Then will you direct it?" Sue asked. "We've got eight under-twelves. Both your fans want to be in it."

Anne sighed. "That Judy – but they do love the water. My cousins and I learned to swim in that pool; we went every day, too. Judy's turning into a good little diver, have you noticed? I've been coaching her." She listened to the music again. "The little kids could swim a simple procession, if they don't all want to be the bride. Aren't there going to be any boys in the show?"

Sue shook her head. "Not in the water ballet. They all want to be clowns. Those guys wouldn't be caught dead doing synchronized." She stood. "Are you ready for another beer?"

Anne nodded, "Please."

Sue paused in the doorway. "The diving team is doing an exhibition and some comic diving during the intermission. Mostly comic if I know that bunch. A lot of boys work on farms during the summer

– especially when the crops come in. They practice after sundown." Sue went into the kitchen. Anne could hear the refrigerator open and close. Outside it was completely dark. Anne walked to the screen door and looked out. The air felt cool and the lighted room behind her was hot. Beyond the shadowed porch the sky was heavily spattered with late-July constellations.

Of course, she thought. But I'd forgotten. The sky was always full of stars in July. When I was a Camp Fire Girl, we used to lie on our backs on the lawn, looking at constellations through a black cardboard telescope from Woolworth's. I never look at the sky in New York. There are too many lighted windows. The buildings channel us.

She heard Sue behind her. "I wonder if the older girls would listen to you – you've just come from the city." Sue was pouring beer from a frosted can into Anne's glass. A head of foam rose, spilling over the rim. Anne bent quickly and sipped a mouthful of suds to stop the swell.

"Sorry," Sue said.

Anne wiped the foam from her lips. "It's good and cold."

Headlights flashed against the windows as a car turned into the driveway and continued past the house to the garage.

"There's Al," Sue said. "I hope he won't want to eat right away. He's got to set up the charcoal broiler in the yard."

Anne stirred uncomfortably. Her cotton dress was hopelessly wrinkled and she was feeling light-headed. The car stopped, its door slammed, and they heard footsteps on the back porch. The kitchen screen door rattled on its hinges.

"Anybody home?" Al appeared in the kitchen doorway. He was shorter than Sue and wore a short-sleeved sport shirt without a tie. His colorless hair was clipped in a crew cut. There's Al, Anne thought, and waited for an impression.

"When you and your ex- lived in Greenwich Village," Al said, "tell me, did you meet any queers?" He was spreading mustard over his hamburger and pointed the yellow-tipped knife at Anne.

Anne sat on the floor near the coffee table, which was spread with picnic food: a platter of hamburgers, sliced tomatoes, deviled eggs, pickles in a jar, and a bottle of catsup.

"James and I lived in the South Village," Anne said. "It was a neighborhood – chiefly Italian – you know, families."

Sue and Al leaned forward on the couch. Sue was dishing potato salad onto paper plates. In the corner the record player spun through Al's collection of old rock-and-roll 45s.

Al speared a tomato with his knife, dropped it onto the hamburger, and snapped the roll shut. "But what about the queers?" he insisted. "Homosexuals?"

"Well," Anne looked around for her beer glass. It was on the floor behind her. "They have their own bars, 'gay' bars."

"The bars in New York are open until four a.m.," Al said. "You can't tell me things don't go on."

"I can't. Things do go on – it's New York."

She looked at Al's flushed face.

"I don't go to the Village anymore," Anne said. "I live up near Columbia now – that's a long subway ride alone at night. The IRT after midnight is my idea of hell. I don't need that."

Al got to his feet and walked around the table. "S'cuse me, Anne, I've got to go take a leak. How about another beer?"

Sue looked embarrassed. "I hope you don't mind the questions. Al's never been anywhere... so he's terribly curious. Nothing ever happens here." She wiped some catsup off the table. "Doesn't anyone see you home?"

Anne shook her head. "I won't let them. It's too far. If I want to see our old friends or have a drink, I know I'll have to take care of myself."

"Al would never let me do that," Sue said. "In the end I guess that's why I married him. Al takes care of me. In Dayton, he used to pick me up every day after school, because of the neighborhood. Al's not exactly educated, but he's very reliable."

The record player changed and a new 45 clicked into place.

Sue emptied a can of beer into her glass and watched it drip. "Al's very reliable."

Outside someone mounted the steps. Anne and Sue looked toward the screen door. A tall woman crossed the porch, reflected in the light from the living room. She had clipped hair and wore a golf dress and brown tie shoes. Behind them, Al returned from the kitchen, carrying two cans of beer.

"Well, well," he said, coming into the room and setting the cans on the coffee table. "If it isn't our friendly landlady."

"Al," Sue warned. Her freckled upper lip stretched, whitening above her mouth.

The woman opened the screen door and walked in. She was as tall as Sue.

"Mother," Sue said, "Hi. I'd like you to meet my new friend, Anne Martin."

Anne tried to stand but her leg cramped and she ended up on her knees.

"Then you must be Mrs. Martin," the woman interrupted. "Your aunts on Elm Street telephoned me just now. They didn't know my daughter's married name," she glanced at Al.

"Mom lives just down the street," Sue explained.

"Alma and Fredonia Reade," Mrs. Fuller said. "I knew your Aunt Alma when she worked at the courthouse. They seem to think you should have been home before this."

Still kneeling, Anne looked at her watch. "It's eleven," she said. She was conscious of wrinkles across her skirt and grease spots from the hamburger where her lap had been.

"Would you like a beer, Mom?" Sue asked.

Mrs. Fuller smiled at Anne. She turned to Sue, "No, honey, I haven't time. Your dad and I are playing bridge with the Hoveys. I said I'd be right back." She looked at Anne. "Your aunts seem quite upset. They said you didn't tell them you'd be out late."

"Late?" Anne managed to rise to her feet. "But it isn't late. I'm awfully sorry that you were bothered, Mrs. Fuller."

The older woman opened the screen door. "We'll see you tomorrow for supper, Sue?" she asked. The door closed and her health shoes sounded on the wooden porch.

"Good grief," Anne said. She stood in the middle of the room. "I'm so sorry, Sue. This is ridiculous. I've got a key… and Wapak's safe. I've been on my own for years now. All alone the last two. I always go home by myself at night – much later than this – and nobody gives a damn. Wapak's nothing compared to New York. Why some of the things I've seen in the subway would make Sodom and Gomorrah look like Disneyland."

"Hey, now, take it easy," Al said. "Have another beer, Anne. Sit down. You can't let these old Wapakoneta biddies run your life. Relax. Drink your beer."

Behind her a porch light flicked off, leaving Anne alone in the black-green quiet. Anne started down the walk. Overhead the dark, arched branches of trees shadowed the pavement from the streetlight.

The air was still. Her sneakers sounded on the cement and she could hear insects under the trimmed grass. Most houses were dark; a few had light in an upstairs window. Anne walked steadily. I'm drunk, she thought. Fireflies lighted in the branches overhead, flickered silently, moving above the still lawns and the black shape of bushes. "Lightning bugs," she explained. There was no one in the street.

At the intersection of Auglaize and Elm streets, the traffic signal was switching colors, although no traffic waited. Anne's eyes fastened on it as she walked. The small circles changed: red: green: yellow. On the far corner someone had left a neon sign lighted in the saloon window: "Frankenmuth Beer." Frankenmuth Beer was brewed in Findlay, Ohio. Anne stopped and waited at the curb for the signal to change before she crossed in the merging arcs of two street lamps, then it was dark again. As she walked toward the black angle of the bridge she began to smell the river.

Underfoot the surface changed; her steps became hollow and metallic – she could see the dark shapes of the banks on either side. The water was not far below. Frogs bellowed across the water to each other, croaked deeply in the tall blurred grass.

Anne stopped and leaned over the rail, breathing the heavy river smell as it rose. The air felt warm and moist. I'm all alone, she thought. She looked down, listening to the water. "James," she said to the water. Her voice seemed to travel a long way downstream. The water flowed. "Damn you, James," she said. "Where are you?" The frogs stopped croaking. She could hear her voice moving downstream. Someone was crying. Anne looked downriver where the banks, dark sky, and water merged. James is asleep, she thought. She stood swaying. At the edge of the water there was a splash. Grass rustled. There was another plop directly below her, near the pilings. Anne leaned far over trying to see into the black water. "OK," she called. "Let's go, gang. Everybody out of the pool."

There was movement in the bank grass, then all was still. She frowned. "Those frogs are a stubborn race," she said and turned away from the rail. Her footsteps continued hollowly. She listened to the sound until it grew thick and solid once more – and then forgot.

The house looked dark as she approached from Elm Street, then she saw a glow along one corner. They had left the porch light on for her. Anne crossed the soft black grass and mounted the wooden steps. She carefully opened the screen door and eased through, holding the hook, trying not to let it bang.

Overhead the hall light went on suddenly. She saw her aunts standing at the foot of the stairs. Both were in their nightgowns and their heads were covered with little gray snails of hair wound on kid curlers and tied. Exactly the same as her grandmother had worn. Alma's glasses glinted octagonally, reflecting the dim overhead light.

"Emma Anne," Alma came forward. "It's midnight. You worried us. We've been waiting up for you."

"You walked home alone," Doe said. "We saw you. Emma Anne, you can't be too careful. The fair is in town."

Anne woke in her grandmother's bed, feeling her head ache. Turning on the pillow she slitted her eyes, letting the bright, hot sunlight under her lashes. Alma was standing in the doorway.

"Emma Anne, the last mass today is at ten-thirty. Fredonia and I let you sleep. We went to the seven as usual. You'll have to get up right away. It's a high mass," Alma added.

Anne felt sweat trickle along her hairline. Fibers of pain branched up the back of her neck, through her right eye, and deep into her skull like a crack. Her mouth was dry. There was no air in the room.

She started to raise her shoulders from the bed and then let her forehead sink back into the hot feather pillow. Hangover, she thought. Oh golly.

Alma turned and left the room.

From the wall the Sacred Heart looked down in agony and distaste at the bed.

Anne pulled herself up leaning on her arms and was suddenly dizzy. Her head fell forward; long hair covered her eyes. Good God, I'm still drunk, she thought. I've got to get out of here. Last night's dress lay over the rocking chair; she'd slept in her underclothes. Anne crawled from the bed and stepped into the wrinkled dress. Trying to pull up the zipper in back, she retched. I can't, she thought. She held onto the bedpost and slipped into her sandals. Doe's hat was on the dresser where it had been put out for her. Anne set the prickly brown nest atop her head and looked in the mirror. "Crowned with thorns," she said. Saliva rose under her dry tongue and her stomach shook. "I can't," she explained to the mirror. She picked up her grandmother's hairbrush, toppling snapshots, and tried to pull it through her tangled hair. The bristles caught in the veiling. "Can't," she said, dropping the brush. "I have to go."

At the foot of the stairs, Alma was waiting with a black Sunday missal. Its spine was misshapen with holy pictures between the pages. Narrow ribbons in liturgical colors trailed out the bottom.

"The tenth Sunday after Pentecost. You'll have to walk fast, Emma Anne."

Anne took the missal stiffly, not daring to look up, and pushed out the screen door. It swung wide on its hinges and banged sharply after her.

The dry heat burned the air around her, and she came from under the trees onto a bare stretch; the sun reflected in glaring layers off the cement. Her eyes burned and she wished she had her sunglasses. I haven't even got my purse, she thought. She walked quickly, trying to get out of sight of the house. Her head was cracking open like split fruit under the hot circle of straw.

Jesus, Mary, and Joseph, she thought, why did this have to happen? She felt the crack widening through her right eye. Saliva was running freely under her tongue. I've got to hurry, she told herself. They won't know; I've got an hour. Sweat began to loosen in all the tight crevices of her body. Ahead she saw the bridge. Its bright metal spurs glared silver under the bright blue sky. Houses and trees stopped, although the cracked sidewalk continued upward toward the bridge. Anne turned off into the dry grass and plunged down through the weeds. Their yellow spikes scratched her legs as the ground sloped away under her feet. Fuzzy stalks of milkweed brushed her bare arms and cracked, oozing sap. The ground continued to drop and the weeds rose. She plunged on down the bank toward the river. White foamy spittle on the joints of green blades flecked her legs and wrists. Insects buzzed around her hair. She could see the brown water ahead. Anne stumbled down the bank and fell onto her knees. She crawled the remaining feet and stretched, flattening the weeds, legs slanting upward, her face inches from the water. Mud streaked the heel of her hand. Far across the river, she heard church bells ring out. Mass was beginning at St. Joseph's. Water flowed slowly past the bent bank grass. Insects rose off the weeds and swarmed above the water. She saw the brown mud lying below the surface. The bells called far above the visible waves of heat. Anne closed her eyes and vomited into the river. She was still wearing her hat.

On Wednesdays, they always baked. The kitchen smelled of warm butterscotch; Alma's pie was in the oven, its stiff peaks of meringue browning. Anne sat at the kitchen table; she had a bag of peas to shell. In front of her stood a colander. Her face was sun-flushed from an afternoon's swimming and her damp bangs made a cool frame over her forehead. The flat pods cracked, splitting open as her fingers moved. The hard pale peas lay in rows, hooked to their pods by tiny umbilicals. They pinged and bounced as she loosened them into the colander.

"I haven't shelled peas in a long time," she said to Alma, who was flouring the steak for Swiss, pounding in flour with the edge of a dinner plate. Doe, home from work, was resting her feet, peeling potatoes across the table.

"I'm going to miss your cooking. In New York, I live on frozen food and yogurt."

"If you don't take care of yourself," Doe said, "you'll get sick and have to pay doctors' bills."

Alma turned, holding the floury plate in her hand. "So you're still determined to go back?"

"Yes, after Labor Day," Anne answered. "I've promised to see the show through. Only three more weeks. They need me and I've got a lot of ideas for the kids' routines. Anyway, I've always loved swimming outdoors. I suppose it's childish, but when I'm swimming I feel as if nothing has ever changed. It's just like our childhood visits. Besides swimming is awfully healthy," she added, "and summer is so short."

"It lasts too long to suit me," Doe said. "I can't take this heat."

"New York isn't a safe place for a woman to live alone," Alma said. "The things we've read... " She wiped her hands on a towel. "You cause your parents anxiety, Emma Anne. Your mother is heartbroken. She isn't well and your dad is getting on. They pray for you to come home. They have no one up there in Akron."

Anne held her breath, shaking; the peas pinged furiously into the colander. "Alma, Mother has chronic sinus and lots of friends. Dad is only fifty-eight. They have each other. Look, Alma, I know I'm a disappointment to them; you don't have to tell me. Everyone is ashamed of me. I'm sorry I'm the only one. They always wanted more children, and now it looks as if they won't have any grandchildren."

Doe looked up across the table. "You can't remarry," she said quietly. "The church forbids it."

Anne's fingers moved angrily. "Perhaps if I did have a husband like Lou and Ev, you'd stop treating me like this."

"You don't act the right way," Alma said. "Leaving a good home. Why do you want to live all by yourself now?"

"I can't live at home and be my parents' child," Anne protested. "I can't fill their need for grandchildren and stay home all my life – just so they can have someone to love and 'do' for. Alma, I have to make something of my own life now. I may be alone for a long time. I might as well get used to it. I manage fine."

Her aunt bent, taking the pie out of the oven. Its warm, brown-sugar smell filled the kitchen. Alma carried it to the lead sink and faced Anne, perspiring from the heat. "Your parents worry that you neglect your religion in New York."

Anne gripped the colander. What's the use, she thought. I can't tell them that I no longer believe anything. I haven't for a long time. They're the lucky ones not to go down screaming. They plan to live forever – up there with my grandmother – quietly stocking their pantry shelves against heaven. Unafraid.

"No one thinks the divorce was your sin," Doe said quickly. "James went back on his promise to the church."

"The church has nothing to do with it," Anne said. "It was my fault, too. You can't blame James." But I do, she thought. "James wasn't *Catholic*, Doe. Besides, he met someone else." Anne looked at both aunts defiantly. "I wanted my freedom," she lied. "I needed it for my work."

"Ambition is a sin," Alma said. "What makes you think that you're any better than the rest of your family? We never wanted to live in New York. We are satisfied with the lives God gave us."

"Jesus Christ, Alma… ," Anne cried.

"That's blasphemy and I won't have it in this house, Emma Anne. You make our Blessed Lady weep."

Two evenings later, Anne stood in the kitchen after supper ironing white net between sheets of waxed paper to make it waterproof. Fredonia was stirring a pan of fudge sauce on the stove for their evening ice cream. "Be sure you clean that iron when you finish, Emma Anne, so it won't scorch the next time we use it."

Anne nodded.

"This is costing you a lot of money," Fredonia said. Her spoon scraped loudly against the sugary pan.

"If my ideas work, Bob's going to get the Park Department to reimburse me." Anne set the iron on its stand.

"Well," Fredonia said, "they certainly aren't paying you for your time."

Anne grinned. "That's show biz."

The second week in August was cold. The kids brought sweaters and shirts to wear over their bathing suits. They shivered, waiting to go into the water. Wet, their tanned skins faded and their lips bleached. Then the week before Labor Day, the weather turned hot again, and Bob called practice for seven a.m.

The first-aid room was stacked with costumes, and the older girls sat on the cots sewing fishnet stockings onto their bathing suits. They had bought big brass curtain rings at the hardware store, which they planned to use as earrings. Both of the spare ring buoys on the wall were strung with tiaras of red and orange plastic roses.

"They're going to look more like gypsies than Puerto Ricans," Sue said as they left the first-aid room. "I just hope they don't sink under all that weight. Bob told me the photographer from the *Wapakoneta News* is coming to the pool this afternoon to take pictures."

Anne slid her dark glasses on over her eyes. The early reflection off the water was dazzling; the pool glimmered and the chlorine smelled fierce.

At the deep end, two boys and a girl were diving, playing the board, chasing each other, springing flat-footed. Anne recognized the girl and grinned; that imp, Judy. The child saw her and waved frantically from the high platform. They were practicing standard comic dives: the one-legged jackknife, riding the horse, dying swan. Daring each other. Anne waved back.

"It looks as if the divers got here early to grab the deep water," Sue said. "Could you rehearse your gang in the shallow for a while? I want to put 'I Feel Pretty' through another land drill anyway. We'll give the divers ten more minutes. I've called 'Maria' for nine."

Over the bathhouse loudspeaker, a phonograph needle scratched in loud decibels as the locker-room attendant put a record on the sound system.

"Ouch," Anne groaned. "That split the air." She looked up at the heat-clogged sky. "America" blasted across the pool. Children began straggling out of the bathhouse. Ginny and a child named Lucy came prancing across the hot cement, round stomachs water-streaked from a fast dodge through the showers.

"Ginny," Anne called, "can you girls bring me the top hats from the first-aid room? We'll practice swimming in them again."

She and the older girls were on the deep-end deck; Sue gesturing, putting them through their formations. The divers continued their manic descents off the high board. Over the music, Anne could hear the board snap and vibrate on its fulcrum. She lined her swimmers in pairs, the taller child of each set wearing a plastic top hat, and sent them swimming back and forth across the shallow end, arms moving in unison. She was at the point of dispatching someone to play their music over the loudspeaker, when she looked up.

Her trained eyes saw at once, and she was running up the side of the pool toward the deep end before she was sure it really happened; a girl's body being flung against the pool edge under the high board, awkwardly striking the cement, sliding down into the water, limp, bumping against the overflow gutter. Water closed over her head. Judy!

Anne ran. Her eyes blurred as her bare feet pressed the hot cement. At the deep end, she saw Sue and another girl dive. Anne rounded the corner by the ladder and reached the poolside under the board as Sue broke the surface, bringing Judy up with her. Water streamed off both faces.

Sue gasped and kicked, holding the child's head above water with both hands. They were only feet away. Anne dropped flat on the cement and stretched over the water to help. The second girl surfaced nearby: Joanie.

She carefully held Judy's chin, hands on either side of the jaw. The child's slack body floated to the surface.

Anne dropped her arms into the water to support the child's shoulders.

"Don't lift," Sue gasped. "I think she struck her spine."

Together they floated the unconscious body parallel to the

poolside.

"She's broken her back," Joanie wailed, sobbing and treading water.

Anne stretched one hand under Judy's head and with the other supported her torso. Sue gripped the overflow gutter with her free hand.

One of the boy divers stretched out beside Anne to keep the child's hips afloat. Joanie held the girl's legs against the poolside.

Anne looked down at the unconscious face floating below her own. Judy's short, dark bangs washed back in the water, and her hair floated about her ears. She was a fair child, under her tan. Her eyelids were slitted and Anne could see the pupils, very black. Water beaded over the lashes.

"She wasn't down long enough," Anne said. "But, Sue, Judy isn't breathing."

Sue, inches away, white and wet, looked scared. Some of the older girls and little kids crowded in, standing over Anne.

Sue shouted to them, "Get Bob. Ellen, call a doctor."

Anne turned her head quickly. "Stay back," she ordered. She bent, remembering, and carefully opened the floating child's jaw. Judy's head bobbed in the water. Sue moved her arm to support the child's neck.

I've got to get it right, Anne thought. She reached both arms over the edge, tilting Judy's chin upward to open the air passage. With her right hand, she pinched the small nostrils between two fingers in a clothespin grip, then scrunching further over the poolside, Anne took a breath and sealed her mouth over the child's open lips. They were cold and wet. She breathed hard into the moist passage and her breath met no resistance. Take it slower, she thought. Watch to see if her chest moves. She glanced at Judy's navy-blue tank top; water floated across it and Judy's peach nose clip bobbed on its rubber band. Anne couldn't tell if the air was helping. Her own chest ached and her breathing was too fast. The sun burned her shoulders; her heart pounded against her ribs crushed into the cement. Judy's head kept floating away. Anne tried to steady it. The child's face was slippery. Her nose and forehead held traces of white cream – the thick, sticky kind lifeguards use to screen out sun. The zinc smell of it mixed with the strong chlorine and baby oil on the girl's chest and arms.

Anne lifted her face to let the air escape, then bent again. Twelve to fifteen times a minute. Count five between breaths, she reminded herself. Slow down.

In the water, Sue supported the child's shoulders, holding onto the overflow gutter. "She's taking air," Sue said, "but I had her up in seconds; it must be her back."

The water glimmered in the sun; the black shadow of the high diving board stretched out over the blue water, shortening as the sun mounted. Anne closed her eyes and tried to concentrate. Inhale, exhale. She could hear the water slosh-sloshing against the poolside. Joanie, still supporting Judy's legs, was snuffling and breathing hard.

Judy trusted me, Anne thought. I've got to keep her breathing. She opened her eyes and looked at the child's face – so close she could see drops of water lying in Judy's partly open eyes, the brown freckles beneath the tan. The eyes were wrong!

Anne felt a hand on her shoulder. Bob was stooping beside her and she saw the pant legs and sneakers of a locker-room boy.

"We're going to lift her, Anne," Bob said. "Keep her back straight. We've got to get her out of the water."

Anne nodded and breathed into the mouth between her hands.

"I'll give you the signal when we're ready." Bob slid his arms underwater beneath the girl's shoulders.

The locker-room boy and one of the divers were getting their arms into position further down – the body moved in the water.

Anne clutched the upturned chin, feeling her mouth slide away, breaking the seal. She lifted her head to let air escape.

"Now," Bob said. They bent and hoisted. Anne let go quickly and slid back, scraping her chest on the cement. The boys lifted Judy out of the pool. She sagged slightly and her head rolled to the side as they lay her flat on the deck.

Anne pushed in quickly, straightening Judy's head and lifting her small chin. She had counted to seven already. Anne sealed her mouth over Judy's open lips, forcing in air. The child's wet face was touching her own; a drop of blood oozed out of the corner of one eye. God, Anne thought, internal. She looked quickly at the ears. No blood. But her fingers were staining around Judy's nostrils. Bob, kneeling beside her, was taking Judy's pulse. Anne heard him send the locker-room attendant for blankets. Sue and Joanie were swimming toward the ladder. Anne raised her face: "A doctor?" and resumed resuscitation.

"They're on the phone," Bob said. "Look, Anne, we're going to need the ambulance. Can you keep it up for a few more minutes? I'll be right back." She could hear him run down the deck.

Anne glanced up. The children were still standing back along the poolside watching; Ginny was crying. Sue and Joanie were comforting them. Anne closed her eyes against the glare of the water; sun pressed hotly on her back.

Sue knelt by Anne. "Ginny says she's her cousin. Joanie's gone to call the family."

Anne looked at the pale face between her hands, but there was no sign. Behind her, the boys returned with some blankets. Anne moved mechanically, beginning to feel dizzy from exhaling too forcefully. Her ears rang and the light fragmented across the bright water. She closed her eyes again to concentrate. How much time had passed?

Sue moved about, covering Judy with blankets, wrapping them around her legs, pulling them up over the wet chest and shoulders. Anne opened her eyes. The red drop in the child's eye was growing, congealing into a single bright tear. Anne's fingers on the nostrils were sticky.

Sue knelt beside Anne, watching Judy for signs. Inhale, exhale. She heard Sue move.

"Jesus," Sue said.

Anne looked up – the sunlight broke into grains and cleared. A priest was approaching, walking quickly up the side of the pool: bare-headed, white collar, a black suit absorbing the sun.

"We need a doctor," Anne said, and forced air down the unresisting young throat. Under the blanket, Judy's chest rose. Anne lifted her head again and pleaded, "Get a doctor."

One of the divers, still watching, took her plea for an order and ran toward the locker room to check. Bob was hurrying up the pool deck behind the priest. Anne kept her eyes fixed on the water, trying not to see the blood oozing, so close, from the orifices of the washed, childish face.

Sue moved away as the priest knelt beside the child's head, opening a small pouch. He leaned over and Anne saw his face: sallow with thinning hair and large ears. Their eyes met and Anne glared. "Don't move her," she said, and returned her mouth to the child's open lips. Out of one eye she could see that his black knees were getting wet on the cement. Inhale, exhale.

Now the priest's hand moved near her eyes. Anne saw his black sleeve and hairy wrist. His thumb was bright and gleaming, and she could smell olive oil. The thumb hovered and made a cross on Judy's forehead, marking the white cream, blending chrism with zinc oxide.

They did not mix. He can't anoint her mouth, Anne thought. I won't let him. The priest was muttering rapidly. His knees were soaked.

Anne raised her head. "We need a doctor," she insisted.

Bob was standing beside the priest. He knelt by Anne's side. "Doc Hauser is coming, Anne. I called the ambulance. Doc was on a house call, but we got him. He's on his way. I'll take over now." He bent close, watching the rhythm of her breathing. "Be ready after this one."

Anne nodded. Inhale, exhale… she lifted her head.

"Now," Bob said. She slid back quickly and Bob moved forward, placing his lips firmly over the open mouth. Ellen slipped in beside him and clamped the nostrils shut with one hand. Blood oozed between her fingers.

Anne stood upright. Her arms ached. The priest was closing his pouch. When he rose, his trousers had dark stains at the knees. Anne moved around behind Bob and knelt by Judy's hand, carefully turning it, seeking a pulse. The short stubby fingers with bitten nails were limp – too cold. Anne always had difficulty finding a pulse, but her fingers touched it; the small measured throb alive within the cold flesh.

Don't press too hard, she warned herself. She didn't have a watch. She turned to ask the priest, but he was walking down the pool deck. Ginny and Lucy were running after him; they seemed to know him. Bob's head moved rhythmically. The sun beat down. Time throbbed under her fingers. People had begun to appear outside the wire pool fence and she wondered where they came from. Cars were stopping behind the bathhouse. She heard their doors slamming. Judy's chest moved silently under the sunny blankets.

Ellen knelt, eyes fixed on Bob, trying not to look at the blood seeping between her fingers. Beyond them the expanse of aqua water stretched, empty, clean, and innocent; shading pale toward the bathhouse.

How long? Judy's pulse seemed faint. Anne relaxed her fingers and found it again. The shadow of the diving board shortened toward noon.

She saw the doctor come through the locker-room door. He was in his shirtsleeves, carrying a satchel. Joanie and the locker-room boy ran beside him as he strode up the pool deck.

"Bob," Anne said, "the doctor's here." She lay the child's hand on the cement and backed away to make room.

The doctor pushed in, motioning her further back. He put his hand on Bob's shoulder and drew him away. Ellen scurried back.

"She isn't breathing," Bob said.

The doctor motioned him out of the way.

Anne joined Sue and Ellen under the shadow of the high board, staring at the doctor's back as he pulled the blankets away. She saw Judy's lips turning blue. No, Anne thought, what kind of a doctor is he? She started to move forward, but the doctor had seen enough. He said something sharply to Bob, who knelt and resumed resuscitation.

Beyond the wire fence they saw the ambulance pull up on the grass, and a locker-room boy was opening the equipment gates.

Anne watched as two attendants, also in shirtsleeves, carefully unloaded the wheeled stretcher and the inhalator with its oxygen tank, guiding them through the open gates. There were crowds outside the fence now. People had followed the ambulance.

"They couldn't get hold of her mother," Sue said to Anne. "Joanie called but there was no answer. They finally got her dad, but he works over in Sidney."

The attendants lifted Judy onto the stretcher and placed the mask of the inhalator over her mouth and nose. Bob walked along with the men helping to guide the stretcher out and into the ambulance. The doctor, holding his satchel, climbed in back.

"It looks like a hearse," Anne said. The ambulance was dark gray.

"It's not the hearse," Sue said. "But it does belong to the funeral home. The fire department uses it in emergencies. It takes too long to get an ambulance from the hospital in Lima. We need a hospital... "

They stared after the ambulance as it drove out of sight. Bob closed and padlocked the gates. He looked tired as he came over and took Ellen's arm.

"Doc said she struck her head. It's probably a concussion. She's good and knocked out, but he can't tell anything until they take X-rays. He can't tell how bad."

I should have known, Anne thought. Judy's eyes were too black. Her pupils shouldn't have dilated in the sun. They were all wrong. Aloud she said, "Then we couldn't have done anything for Judy, even if we had known. It wasn't drowning."

"No," Bob said. "We couldn't have done a thing. We kept her breathing." They walked along the dry cement. Bob put his arm around Ellen. Outside, the onlookers began to drift away.

Doe was already home for lunch when Anne walked in. Alma stood at the lead sink, slicing tomatoes. The kitchen table was set. Anne slid into her place at the table. Past Alma, out the back screen door, she could see the midday sun shining on the gray cellar door and the stone cistern cover. In the yard there was a hot, rectangular garden of marigolds, zinnias, and phlox that her grandmother had planted long ago. It ran parallel to the tall wooden T-posts where the clotheslines had always been strung. The weathered posts were far apart. Forty years ago, they had been a large family.

Doe sat down and unfolded her napkin. "Emma Anne, they say

that the little Haines girl almost drowned this morning at the swimming pool. The Farley child, whose mother works in packing, was at the pool. She called her mother at the factory."

Anne looked at her aunt. "It wasn't a drowning," she said. "I was there. It was a diving accident. Judy was clowning and slipped off the board; her momentum carried her back against the cement. They only took her to Lima an hour ago. It took so long to get a doctor. The priest arrived before the doctor did." I was one of the people who kept Judy alive, she thought. I did what I knew how to do. The accident wasn't my fault. "It wasn't anyone's fault," she said.

Alma carried the sliced tomatoes and onions floating in a dish of vinegar to the table. "Edith Farr called us, Emma Anne. She heard in town that there'd been a drowning at the pool this morning. She wanted to know if you knew who it was."

"I saw her hit the cement before she went into the water," Anne said. "Judy was unconscious when they brought her up. We waited – it seemed like forever – for help." Anne stared at the bright, distinct flowers beyond the screen door. Tall purple cosmos with yellow centers like daisies had thrust up in patches, spiked and insistent above the zinnias. She remembered her grandmother standing behind the zinnias. Her grandmother always wore a sunbonnet cutting flowers: a limp blue mobcap, more like a cabbage than a sun shade. I was the only adult at the pool, Anne thought, and Sue... but Sue belongs here. There were once morning glories climbing on the clothes-posts, and she wondered what had happened to them. This shouldn't have happened here – not here. Terrible things happen in New York. I'm responsible, she thought. I wanted to go back – just for a little while – to forget everything that happened to me. I wanted to be safe again. The way I used to be. But only for a few months. They did need me at the pool. They liked me. My mistakes followed me. I bring harm.

Am I responsible because they liked me? Anne looked straight at both aunts. "Mrs. Farr is a busybody," she said. "Judy Haines was alive when she was taken from the pool. I know – I had a pulse that whole time."

By three she had paced in and out of the house four times – laying her library book on the porch swing, walking back and forth across the flowered dining-room carpet to the kitchen for lemonade, paging through the Sears catalogs on the hall table. Alma was making tomato preserves. She looked up as Anne went to the refrigerator again. The red, seedy pulp bubbled on the stove. Alma added sugar.

"I think I'm going to walk over to the pool," Anne said, "to see if there's any news."

"Why can't you just telephone?" Alma asked.

"I don't want to do that. The phone has probably been ringing all afternoon. Anyway I have to get out. I feel shaky."

"That's the way it is," Alma said. "It always hits you when it's all over."

Anne took the long way back to the pool instead of the river path. As she passed the thinning residential district, houses stopped, the sidewalk ended, and a cornfield began. Anne carefully crossed the road, skirting the town baseball diamond. Her bare feet slid on the dusty grass and she could hear noise from the pool.

When she got there, it was crowded as usual. The older girls were running around the locker room in their costumes; the photographer from the paper had come. Anne had forgotten about the photographer. It seemed to her that after the morning, he should not be there.

Bob was glad to see her. Ellen and Joanie were with him in their stockings and tiaras. "Anne," he said, "put your suit on and get into the pictures."

"No." Anne felt confused. "That's not why I came. Actually I'd forgotten." Did they think she wanted her picture in the paper? She shifted her bare feet on the cool bathhouse floor. "I just stopped... Bob, I wonder if you've had any news?"

His smile was gone. "I called the hospital," he said. "After Judy arrived. They say it's a concussion. I don't know. That doesn't sound too serious – maybe uncomfortable as hell. Judy's father's gone to Lima. They're still trying to bring her round."

Anne breathed slowly – just a concussion – then it wasn't serious. She felt suddenly freed. Her fingers loosened; she hadn't realized they were clenched. "It's going to be all right then," she said simply. "Do you know, I've never had to give respiration before. I was scared."

Bob smiled again. "I don't mind admitting that I was plenty worried until Doc got there. Look, Anne, do you think you could round up that gang of yours with the hats for a photograph. I saw them running into the showers a minute ago."

At eight in the morning, the phone rang. Anne got up from the breakfast table, toast still in her hand, knowing that it was for her. The day was hot already; Doe and Alma had gone to seven o'clock mass. Anne lifted the receiver of the upright telephone on the sideboard. She was standing next to the aged cactus plant on its stand. The long rapier leaves, mottled dark green, were covered with dust. Their edges faded yellow, but the needle points were purple and thick as fingernails.

"Anne." Sue's voice sounded choked at the other end. "Judy Haines died early this morning on the operating table. She never did come to."

"Died?" Anne said. "But we thought – they told us – everything would be all right." She stared at the cactus. It looked as if it were devouring motes of dust suspended in the sunlight that streamed through her grandmother's net curtains. The green blinds were partly drawn to keep the rug from fading.

"You're crying," she said, then, "How's Bob taking it?"

"I think Bob's going to call the show. Mom said he didn't do anything. After Judy's dad called him this morning, he just went up to his room. He's still there. Mom phoned me. I suppose everyone knows by now; this is a small town. The phone's been ringing here ever since – kids asking about practice."

"We thought she was going to be all right," Anne insisted.

"Look, Anne, I have to go. I heard the baby crying. I've got him outside."

"Sue… thanks for calling," Anne said. She hung up and stared at the dust suspended in the sunlight. I shouldn't have come here, she thought.

Anne set the typewriter on the front porch and sat on the swing, paging through her forgotten thesis, trying to get back into her own work. The swing moved slowly. She looked out over the wooden porch rail. The grass was low, still brown from the late-August scorch. Across the street, the big wooden houses stood silent. Anne watched them advance and retreat. Their open screened windows and shadowed doors gaped blackly at the sun. In the living room, Alma turned on her afternoon soap opera. Its nervous, perpetually troubled dialogue floated out to the porch.

Anne turned a corrected page and looked across the street at the vacant windows, wondering if anyone was watching. The pool was still open, although the show had been canceled, but she didn't want to swim. That was over. She thought about the kids and wondered if any of them blamed her. I tried to keep Judy alive, she told herself.

There wasn't anything else I could do.

The dead child had been taken to Kohlers Funeral Home, her aunts had told her. She could be seen that evening. "I've seen her," Anne said. "She had freckles." She looked at the windows across the street and thought she saw a face.

Anne stood quietly and crossed the porch on bare feet. Behind her the thesis swung gently back and forth on the green swing slats. Her feet moved silently across the flaking gray wood, stepped down on the cool chill of shaded cement, touched sudden warmth where the sun began. She walked around the house to the backyard. The grass was dry and dirt sifted between her toes.

Here the air smelled of dropped pears rotting in the grass beneath the pear trees. Her grandmother's flowers, blooming in the long center patch, were faded with heat. Dying zinnias on thick stalks showed brown undersides to the sun. Parched asters bowed their withered heads. A rich fume of decaying fruit drifted on the hot air. Anne walked to the far side of the flower bed and sat on the grass, tightly clasping her knees. Why am I so scared? she thought. Sun blazed above the dying flowers and a wasp circled, drawn by the fetid pears. The dry hollyhocks were full of small insects. Anne lowered her head on her knees and closed her eyes. What's the use, what is the use? It follows me like a sin. Good no longer happens. I bring pain. She held her legs tightly, curling her toes, and forced her eyes open. The sun was dangerously bright. Anne made herself stare at the house. It stood, white clapboard lined by sun shadows, tall and worn. Long black windows, uneven steps, sloping cellar door. The light glared.

I'm losing hold. She sat hunched in the grass looking at the house. No one would know what to do. Her parents would only be hurt again, wondering why such things happened. Their prayers, she knew, were never answered. The stalks of the high flowers cast striated shadows across the grass onto her legs. She stared past the brown petals, feeling the heat that faded them. Because I lost James, I lost my family, too. I injure people, and now I've killed that child. "Nonsense," she said aloud. "It was an accident." The heat shimmered on the unmoving air. I can't break down. No one would understand. No one would know what to do. There's no one to forgive me. Anne raised her face until the sun hurt her eyes.

The house stood silent in the sun; heat shone visibly above the sere flowers. Anne sat very still on the grass, clasping her knees.

The aunts walked her to the train. They took the back way along the other bank of the river, under trees, over the footbridge, and through a sunny field of wildflowers behind the station.

Anne had not wanted them to come. The midday sun was hot and high. Alma sweated, mopping her face every few feet, shifting the cardboard box that held the lunch they had packed for her. Doe walked sturdily along the dirt path, toeing out in her white health shoes, slope-shouldered, carrying a shopping bag full of ripe tomatoes for Anne's parents in Akron. They came single file through a field of yellow weeds. Anne in the lead, dragging her suitcase. Grasshoppers, perched like brown buds, bowed down the wheaty stalks and sprang across the narrow path, whirring.

"Nasty things," Doe said. "Spitting tobacco. It means an early winter."

Anne pushed the dry stalks out of their way with her suitcase. The sun warmed the crown of her head. She looked back at her aunts. "There's a fable for you, Doe – the aunts and the grasshopper. Fall is here and I've nothing to show for my summer. Your pantry shelves are filled with canned pears and tomatoes against the winter."

Behind her, Alma said, "Emma Anne, I've put three quarts of pears and a glass of jelly in this box for your dad; he always liked our spiced pears."

Anne smiled to herself and swept at the weeds with her suitcase. She could see trimmed grass by the station house and an empty wooden bench not far from the tracks. The only other passenger was a man in a work shirt and Levi's, who waited under the station overhang. He had no luggage. Anne set her suitcase on the grass and took the shopping bag from Doe.

Alma looked at her watch. "Not a minute to spare," she said. Sweat glistened below her glasses on both white cheeks.

Anne looked down the tracks; telephone poles stretched beside the rails, their wires stringing into the horizon.

"We're sorry you wouldn't stay Labor Day to see Mary Lou and Jack. They always drive up on a long weekend." Doe wiped her face.

"It's been too long," Anne said. "We wouldn't know what to say." They could hear the train far off. Anne put the tomatoes on the bench and hugged both aunts. Doe, narrow and bony, smelling of glycerin and rosewater. Alma, shorter, a pliant roundness, the sour, dumpling smell of the kitchen. Moist. She wouldn't see them for a long time. The train rushed into the station. "We'll pray for you, Emma Anne," Alma said.

"Yes," Doe added, "now be sure and write to us."

Anne handed up her suitcase to the conductor and grasped the metal rail. Doe gave her the shopping bag and lunch.

"Give our love to your mom and dad."

Inside, the train smelled of hard candy and plush. Anne found an empty seat by a window and hoisted the suitcase above it, then looked out the streaked glass. As the train pulled away, both aunts were waving. She watched them diminish, standing there in the sunlight. The train moved slowly over the railroad bridge where the yellow river stretched along its dark green banks. She felt her throat tighten, and her eyes blurred. The train picked up speed. Anne pressed her forehead against the window and watched the river, the trees, the low buildings of Wapakoneta disappear.

New York is a city of neighborhoods. I returned to the one I knew best, Morningside Heights on Manhattan's Upper West Side, where I had started as a grad student. At night, from my apartment windows, I could see the Palisades light up as the sky darkened above the Hudson River. That was the summer of the war with New Jersey.

THE WAR WITH NEW JERSEY

"ARE WE WINNING? Are we winning, Anne?" Kevin tugs at my hand excitedly. It is a hot July afternoon and we are walking along the esplanade of Riverside Drive. Kevin is dirty, his cotton shorts too long above his four-year-old legs; my sneakers have seen better days. Ahead of us rises that tall Athenian temple, the Soldiers' and Sailors' Monument at 89th Street; its decorated marble dome juts white in the sun above the park. We pause under the trees, Kevin looking up at me. His face needs washing.

"Winning what?"

"The war, the war. Are we beating them?"

I am puzzled and follow his gaze. Below the monument, spaced along the stone esplanade wall, are three black and shiny Civil War cannons, their muzzles angled over the Hudson, pointing toward

Jersey. On the other side of the river stands Edgewater, gray and desolate. Defeated?

"Oh, the war," I say. "The war with New Jersey? Yes, we're giving them a terrible beating."

At night on the Fourth that summer, Macy's sets off its annual fireworks display from barges in the middle of the Hudson River. I wake a sleepy Kevin minutes before it is to begin, and we take the elevator five floors to the roof of his building, climbing a final short flight of stairs in the dark. On the roof it is black and cool. All around us, piled like building blocks, stretch the square black tops of other buildings. Our roof is the highest in the neighborhood. We cross its asphalt between chimneys and the dark shapes of ventilators. Above, the sky is starry. Soot crunches under our feet. At the far west end we make out four or five people leaning against the guard wall, looking out over the river. I take Kevin's hand as we start toward them. Overhead a rocket bursts white across the sky. Another... then another. Streaking up at angles, bursting as they mount, showering white... pink... green. Set fireworks light up on the barges, and the sky flashes. Above us a popcorn explosion of stars shimmers, leaving their image on the black retina of night over New Jersey as they fade. Kevin's face, turned upward, is illuminated in each flash. Excited, he begins whooping – racing around me in circles on the roof in his seersucker pajamas, waving his arms. Suddenly across the Hudson, answering rockets shoot up out of the Palisades, streaking toward us through the sky, bursting over the river. The sky is filled with Roman candles, crossing in the air. Careening. Exploding.

"Anne, they're shooting at us." Kevin is ecstatic.

We stand together on the black roof looking up. It may be a close war.

That was the summer I met Kevin and Ellen. Their father had recently been divorced by a second wife, after filing for bankruptcy, and had come to New York to look for a job. He was planning to bring his two children, by his first marriage, to the city with him, and had sublet an apartment in an old building a few blocks from where I lived on the Upper West Side. He had gone to college with friends of mine, and I met him with them one night in "our" bar in the Village. When he learned that we were almost neighbors, he invited me over to meet his children. An aunt had been keeping them upstate until he found an apartment, and would be driving them down the following week. Kevin was four and Ellen was seven. He planned to enroll them in one of the city's day care centers.

Earlier that year I had been divorced by my husband, an instructor at Columbia, because he wanted to marry someone else. This fact – deserved or not – shocked me. We were young; we had been married only three years. I no longer felt the world was a reasonable place. I was shocked easily then, and I drank a lot to shock the world back. I did not especially like the children's father, but I said, yes, I'd come to supper. I felt sorry for him. The world was, after all, not a reasonable place.

Although the door to the lobby of the apartment building was wide open to let air circulate, I rang the downstairs buzzer anyway. There was no doorman on duty. It was a hot evening, close in the street, and I could smell pizza wafting from the restaurant around the corner of 108th Street and Broadway. For a second, I had an impulse to just buy a slice and return home, but I had pushed the buzzer and the speaker crackled electronically in response.

"Anne," I shouted into the round grill.

Far inside the sputtering mesh, a voice answered, "Ellen, Kevin... on the way down." He had sent the children to greet me. It was more as if he had released them. They tumbled out of the elevator door as it opened, each trying to be out first, and then stopped abruptly in the lobby to stare. Strange, tanned children in washed T-shirts and unironed shorts: a big girl with long hair and bangs, and a smaller, shaggier boy, recently scrubbed. They stood looking at me, and the girl decided, turning to the boy, "She's the one, Kevin." I was captured and conveyed upstairs.

For a cocktail I was given a tall glass, half lemonade, half cheap sherry, with ice cubes. I found it cold and sweet, and because of the heat I drank it far too fast. We sat around the big dining room table under the amber globes of the chandelier. Dinner was baked macaroni and cheese with hot dogs and supermarket rolls. While the children ate dessert, their father offered to make me another lemonade. Kevin was finishing his cherry vanilla ice cream, attacking the melted mound with a teaspoon clenched in one hand. The paper napkin tied around his neck was growing sticky with pink syrup. I tried not to watch; he spit out the cherries.

"I don't like cherries," he said each time.

Ellen glanced up, "You're disgusting, Kevin." She was drawing at her place, empty ice cream dish pushed to one side, filling yellow copy-sheets with tall, wasp-waisted girls. They had round heads, two-dot noses, little circles at the end of their wrists, and expressions of full, staring disapproval. I was fascinated. I took another ginger snap from Mrs. Shaeffer's pink plate and looked around Mrs. Shaeffer's amber-lit dining room.

I had been told about Mrs. Shaeffer, and at length. The apartment belonged to her and she had lived in it for forty-three years with Mr. Shaeffer, who was no longer well. The couple had sublet for the first time that summer and were visiting out of the city. Mrs. Shaeffer was concerned about her possessions. The dining-room walls were lined with glass-paneled side-boards through which you could see tarnished silverplate, stacks of china, and cut-glass vases. All of these were locked and Mrs. Shaeffer had taken the keys away with her. She had left the kitchen china: five chipped pink plates, three cups, six saucers, some bowls, and an assortment of jelly glasses varying in shape. All of Mrs. Shaeffer's kitchen drawers were full of string, except for the ones that were full of plastic bags.

"It's probably a good thing she locked up her china… " The children's father came back carrying my lemonade just in time to see Kevin's ice cream dish moving across the table as he pursued it with a spoon. His father stopped it inches from the edge. "Still, I don't see that leaving a few glasses actually intended for drinking would spoil us." He handed me my lemonade, ice clinking.

"There's a pink glass in Mrs. Shaeffer's bathroom," Ellen said. Her head was bent over her drawing, long hair hiding her face.

"That's plastic," her father answered.

I leaned toward her, "Can I see your pencil?"

She peered warily from under her bangs, and at a look from her father, handed it to me.

I laughed, "Where did you get this?"

Ellen hesitated, still watching her father… "It was in Mrs. Shaeffer's desk."

He blew up, "I thought I told you and Kevin… "

Kevin attempted to hide behind the pink napkin.

"But look," I interrupted. "It says, 'WIN WITH WILKIE'."

After dinner, I was offered another sherry-lemonade in Mrs. Shaeffer's living room – a very brown living room enlivened by touches of maroon. There was an umber plush sofa against one wall, three

151

arm chairs guarded by standing lamps with holly-hock shades and dangling pull cords, an upright piano with its keyboard cover folded down and locked, a coffee table devoid of ornament, and between two windows that looked out over 108th Street, a desk and chair. Above the desk, filling that space, hung a framed reproduction of Battersea Bridge, a painting that seemed to grow even murkier when the light was turned on. In front of each window stood a three-legged metal plant stand with enormous china pots that held a maiden hair fern and two elderly cactus plants. Mrs. Shaeffer's curtains were net. In the long entry hall, I had seen some bookcases.

I sipped my lemonade, cold and sweet in the warm brown murk of the living room. The plush sofa scratched the backs of my knees. Through the arched entrance of the dining room, I could see Ellen at the table drawing, framed in amber light from the chandelier. When she finished a picture she would bring it in to show us, accept our praise graciously, and go back to do another. Her front teeth were growing back in, creating uneven spaces in her smile. She was big for her age. She tried hard to please.

I was beginning to feel sleepy from the sherry and heat; Kevin kept trying to crawl into my lap.

"Go find something to do," his father told him.

"Can I sit on your lap?" he asked me, starting up.

I was flattered – that he would want to. "It's all right," I told his father.

Kevin kneed himself over my legs and settled happily, facing outward, a look of accomplishment spread across his small up-turned features. His father kept talking. Kevin's sneakers bumped against my kneecaps. With my free hand I shifted him slightly; ice cubes rocked in my glass. Below my chin his scalp smelled warm and doggy, and the back of his tanned neck was moist. I tried to listen to what his father was saying.

". . . so you see, I'm hoist: the job I started last week pays too much to qualify me for city day care – despite the fact that the money's already spent before I earn it. We owe Mrs. Shaeffer a month and security on this landmark, and I have to borrow to pay the employment agency that found me the job... "

I listened sleepily, barely hearing. Kevin squirmed in my lap, jarring my arm – cold lemonade splashed over my wrist. Out in the amber dining room, Ellen chewed thoughtfully on her pencil. Fogged brown night settled over Battersea Bridge.

". . . I tried to enroll them in day camp at the Cathedral – only ten dollars each a week. Ellen's old enough, but they won't take Kevin."

What had he been saying? I jerked my mind back.

"I have to keep this job, so I can't see any way out. Ellen's fairly reliable; I think I can trust her to stay here during the day and watch Kevin, until I can work something out. I can't let them go outside. They don't know the neighborhood yet. It's not like a small town where... "

"She's only seven years old," I protested. "You can't leave... " I stopped myself.

"She'll be eight in August," he said confidently.

I looked away – staring at the old brown furniture – hating him for telling me and making me feel guilty. I had nothing to do that summer. In the fall, I would start working in the Columbia library, taking courses at night, tuition free, until I finished my thesis. I had a cheap apartment, too much furniture, and a number of tarnished wedding presents, still in their white cardboard boxes, on my closet shelves. I was set. I felt very guilty indeed. I wondered if he really might go to work, locking them in the apartment for the day, telephoning Ellen every so often to make sure they were all right. I thought he might. Kevin put a sticky hand on my wrist and bent his head to take a swallow from my glass.

"Hey," I pulled the drink away.

"I like that," he told me.

I glanced at Ellen quietly drawing in the dining room. They had already had two mothers who didn't want them – why must I? Why should I feel guilty? No one wanted me either. In a world of shaking unfairness, we were three losers. In a sudden surge of anger, I decided to want them. To hell with everyone else. "All right," I said, "I'll do it." Of course, this was exactly what I had been intended to offer. That had been what the dinner and sherry were all about. "But," I added, "*only* until you find some place… or someone else." It did not occur to me, then, that, since I had made such a shambles of my own life, I was not the happiest choice to straighten out anyone's children. There simply wasn't anyone else. I was better than nothing.

The next morning I wasn't at all confident. My head hurt. I felt sick. And when I slit my eyes to let the sunlight filter under my lashes, the pain nearly blinded me. I rolled over and tried to go back to sleep, but the phone rang.

"I thought I'd make sure you were up," he said cheerfully. "I'm feeding the kids their breakfast now. I need to leave soon."

I leaned my forehead against the wall and tried to stand upright. "I was just leaving," I said.

The door closed; we heard the elevator going down. Ellen, Kevin, and I were alone in Mrs. Shaeffer's apartment. I turned to look at them – they had begun to circle like strange animals waiting for me to make the first move. I wasn't sure what it was. In the kitchen I could see breakfast dishes still on the table. Sunlight streamed through the open window over the pink bowls, soggy with milk and cornflake residue, and slanted hotly against a carton of milk that had been left out. I was pleased to have found some simple, domestic act to establish my authority.

"First, we do the dishes," I said. They trailed me into the kitchen, coming closer to watch. I picked up the bowls, intending to carry them to the sink. A yellow sheet of Ellen's drawings, clinging to the underside of one bowl, came unstuck and fluttered to the linoleum. I stopped to pick it up. Out of the corner of my eye, I saw Kevin's hand reach out, then everything blurred. I straightened in time to see my glasses sail out Mrs. Shaeffer's kitchen window, eight stories above the ground.

"Kevin!" Ellen shouted.

"I don't like glasses," he said.

I looked. I just looked. He smiled up at me confidently. I couldn't believe it. Sun continued to stream through the open window. Ellen watched me.

"Okay," I decided quickly, taking Kevin by the arm. "We're going downstairs and pick up the pieces. You too," I told Ellen – I was afraid to let anyone out of my sight. "We're all in this together." I grasped both of them by the arm, and hurried them out of the apartment and into the elevator, keeping a firm grip as we came out of the building onto 108th Street.

"You're hurting me," Ellen complained.

"Sorry," I answered, releasing her. Morning sun glanced off the parked cars along the curb. At the corner, on Broadway, traffic hummed. I had a sudden vision of these children witlessly dashing themselves under speeding wheels to thwart me. "Stay on the sidewalk," I ordered.

Ellen stared at me.

Keeping hold of Kevin, I started down 108th Street. His short legs pedaled over the cement. I saw my glasses ahead, still lying on the pavement where they had landed, not far from the building. They were open, resting on their shell rims. We stopped and stared down at them; the lenses were unbroken – intact. I picked them up with relief. I was not going to have to punish anyone. Seeing me relax, Ellen smiled. I put the glasses on and looked down at Kevin, standing very small on the sidewalk in his unlaced sneakers.

"You were very lucky," I said.

He looked at the pavement.

"Do you have any idea what would have happened to you if these glasses had been broken?"

Kevin shook his head, then looked up at me. "What?" he asked, suddenly interested.

I stopped. I didn't know. I glanced at Ellen. She was waiting too. "Something… unspeakable," I said. "Truly unspeakable. We're very lucky."

The days were long, hot ones on the Upper West Side, boring indoors and sticky out. We spent afternoons in the apartment with the sounds of traffic coming through the open window. Dust motes floated in the sun over the rug where we lay on our stomachs and played dominoes. Or Ellen would draw at the dining-room table, while Kevin made complex structures out of building blocks in the living room, never able to resist the hubris of adding just one more. We would hear the sound of wooden blocks collapsing, plocking one against the other, and then, the whole tower would give way, toppling amid his howls. Roaring with disappointment, inconsolable. He never learned.

Often we would go to the park, walking down the eroded slopes toward the highway and river, over burnt grass and discarded bottles; or north toward Columbia, past summer school students in shorts entwined on blankets... "Kevin come back here! Kevin!"... or south, where playgrounds, swings, and baseball diamonds covered flat ground. Ellen made friends, but other children always seemed to hit Kevin. He played alone, digging in dirty sand, falling down precipices, or needing to be pushed on the swings – skinny legs, big sneakers, knobby knees, flying out above my head as I leaned for the seat. "Higher, Anne" – silhouetted against the sky. Jerked back, falling toward me, "Higher, Anne."

Other days, we'd walk over the hot city streets to the branch public library at 100th Street. Ellen could read, but owned only one book, *Little Women*, salvaged from their lost house upstate. She proudly signed her name for her own library card. Kevin took books out on my card, which I promised to read to him. On each trip he chose the same orange picture book about a boring, anthropomorphic steam shovel, which I hated. "What about a nice 'Uncle Wiggly'?" I suggested. "Gentleman rabbit... "

"I like steam shovels," he told me.

"Would you want your sister to marry one?" I asked meanly.

Walking home from the library we'd stop at a sidewalk ice cream cart and buy chocolate-covered ice cream sticks that always melted at the bottom faster than you could eat down from the top. We would trudge down the street, carrying our library books and dripping chocolate: dirty, unwanted, and happy as clams.

"Any new diseases, Anne?" Kevin was sitting up in bed in faded seersucker pajamas. Ellen was still brushing her teeth in the bathroom. From Mrs. Shaeffer's back bedroom windows we had a clear view of the sun going down redly behind New Jersey. As it disappeared in a wash of orange and gray, the "Spry" sign further south lit up.

"What does that say?" Kevin demanded. "Read it, Anne."

I looked out the window. "It says, 'We surrender.'"

In the doorway, Ellen gasped open-mouthed at my fib; the points of her bangs were wet and she was wearing a short cotton nightgown. I winked to show her I was joking. Their father's magazine went to press that week and he had called to say he would be working late. We had eaten corned beef hash with catsup for supper, and bought a box of Fig Newtons afterward at the delicatessen for dessert.

"What about a disease?" Kevin asked.

"Wouldn't you rather have a story? Three Bears? Pinocchio? My summer at Camp Fire Girl camp? The time Arthur Moore got arrested for littering?"

He shook his head.

Ellen climbed into bed. "No, a disease," she insisted.

I had begun to worry about what I believed was a morbid streak in them. It had begun the day we saw the torso in a wheelchair on Amsterdam Avenue on our way to the library: a husky male with muscular arms but no legs at all, not even stumps. He was out sunning by the housing project, and seemed to be there every time we walked to the library. I went out of my way not to stare, but Ellen and Kevin liked him, and waved as I dragged them past.

"He waved back," Ellen informed me. They were fascinated.

Suddenly the Upper West Side seemed alive with deformity: cripples, amputees, paralytics, seeing-eye dogs. Hydrocephalic infants and mad old ladies dogged our steps. I worried about Ellen in particular; she was displaying an enormous interest in cripples and orphans. Her drawings were full of children on crutches, children with bandages, little match girls. When we went to the park, she sat under the trees, eyes full of tears, wallowing through *Sara Crewe, Understood Betsy, Heidi, The Secret Garden, Anne of Green Gables.*

"Wait until you read *The Little Lame Prince,*" I promised her. "It's about a *crippled orphan.*"

I had made the mistake of warning Kevin about chasing squirrels by telling him about rabies. Ellen said she had had chicken pox, which led, on succeeding days, to whooping cough, tuberculosis, scarlet fever, ringworm, and warts.

"*Winnie the Pooh?*" I bribed.

"A disease," they said.

I sat on the edge of the bed. "Have we done leprosy?" I asked. They shook their heads.

I reached over and turned off the light. "Well, leprosy," I began, and warmed to my subject.

It was a fiercely hot afternoon, near closing time, at the Museum of Natural History. We sat in the noisy, vaulted, basement cafeteria eating chocolate ice cream from Dixie cups with little wooden spoons. Groups of day camp children swarmed around their counselors, shouting to one another. The table was sticky. Kevin dug into his frozen chocolate thoughtfully. "I like boats," he said to himself. Earlier in the south hall we had come upon a long war canoe, full of dusty, life-size, painted savages. The day camps re-grouped noisily at the doors to depart. I prodded Ellen and Kevin to eat up.

We came down the steps into the slanting five o'clock sun. Its heat scorched the air. On the corner of Central Park West and 83rd Street, a Good Humor cart did steady business.

"I'm too tired," Ellen said. "Let's take a bus."

"The bus is on Broadway," I answered, taking Kevin's hand.

Ellen stopped on the corner. "Then let's take a taxi."

"We don't have enough money. A few more blocks won't kill you."

"Then I want a Good Humor."

"You just finished an ice cream in the museum," I told her.

Kevin looked up at me hopefully. "Can we have a popsicle, Anne?"

"No," I said. "You just had a Dixie cup. You have to go home to supper."

Ellen glared at me. "I'm not going home," she announced, standing feet apart in the sun. Her widely set brown eyes and flat nose lifted in defiance at me. I had put her hair in two pony tails; they jutted out behind her ears as she set her head stubbornly.

"Yes," I said. "We're going home."

Ellen gave me a dirty, seven-year-old look, as if she were going to cry. "You can't tell me what to do. You're not my mother," she said defiantly and sat down in the middle of the sidewalk.

My heart thudded to a halt. It was beastly hot standing in the sun.

I grabbed Kevin's hand before he could sit too, and turned to go, nearly lifting him off the pavement. "We're leaving," I said. "You'd better come too." I started walking up 83rd Street, slow and deliberate, not daring to look back. What if she refused? What if I lost her? I kept walking. What had I done? How could I have been so mean? Two mothers had deserted her, and she knew that.

Beside me Kevin trotted along; I held his wrist firmly. "Is Ellen coming?" I asked him, keeping my face straight ahead.

He looked over his shoulder, stumbled, and shook his head.

We kept walking until we reached the corner and stopped for a light. "Look again," I told Kevin.

"She's coming," he said.

Rather than cross the street, I turned and walked up Columbus Avenue. In the plate glass windows of stores and bodegas, I could see

Ellen slowly following us, half a block behind. I felt sorry for her. She was scared. She did not know the city and was totally dependent on me. She tried so hard to be good.

Ellen stayed behind us, closing the gap a little so as not to lose sight. If she did, she would be lost, and she knew it. We dragged all the way home like that.

The summer passed in steady sunlight and unbelievable heat. We began to go swimming, taking the subway to a small, outdoor city-run pool in the South Village near where I once lived. There, hidden behind brick buildings, Ellen and Kevin splashed in the blue chlorinated city water, and learned to swim. Even the shallow end of the pool was too deep for Kevin. He flung himself, head first, arms and legs outstretched, off the side of the pool into deep water, and held his breath until I grabbed him. Once safe, he clung to my back like a wet rubber band, while I stroked with him across the pool. I had raced free-style for my college team.

"Were you a winner, Anne? A champion?" Kevin demanded.

"Oh, absolutely."

After swimming, we came out of the bathhouse, sunburnt and still dripping, to meet the heavy, hot air and Seventh Avenue cement. Their appetites were boundless after swimming, and I was generally broke. We began stopping in small Village bistros on our way to the subway. Places where the bartenders, who knew me, would give the children free glasses of ginger ale, and where, for the price of my beer, we could eat all the hors d'oeuvres we could grab with both hands. We timed these raids just before the cocktail hour, when the cool, dark little bars were nearly empty. Setting our bathing suits on the butcher-block tables, we crossed the damp, sawdusty floors in search of free food. Ellen and Kevin hated clam dip and spit it out, but they

161

made tall cracker sandwiches out of salami, cheese, and little cocktail wieners. These forays into the free-lunch world shocked my friends. "Can we go to a bar, Anne?" the children would ask in corrupt innocence, thinking of cold ginger ale and the juke box. We were finally eighty-sixed by public opinion.

"I'm calm, Anne. I'm calm." Kevin howled as I immobilized him to control his tantrum. I had just stopped him from violating Mrs. Shaeffer's poor old maidenhair fern; fronds lay beneath its stand on the floor. He had been giving some plastic soldiers a military burial in its pot.

"Are you sure you're calmer?" I asked, holding his arms down, and scissoring his legs with my knees to keep him from kicking. I had always felt that children should never be struck, and expressed strong, idealistic views on this subject. Faced with Kevin, I was not sure what to do. Finally I hit upon the strategy of immobilizing him until he calmed down enough for me to reason with him.

"I'm calmer," he bellowed, tears streaming down the dirt on his cheeks.

"Then stop that dreadful noise right now." I released him. "All right," I said, sitting on a dining-room chair, facing him eye level. "Now you've been told dozens of times not to touch Mrs. Shaeffer's plants, so why were you burying those soldiers in her fern?"

Kevin looked at me through his tears and dirt, and smiled cunningly. "They were dead," he answered.

I reached across and pulled him over my knees, backside up, legs kicking, and whacked him across his shorts with the flat of my hand.

He stopped howling, and looked back at me upside down. "That didn't hurt," he told me defiantly.

"No? Then I'll never tell you about how my Camp Fire troop

all got poison ivy crawling under the Johnsons' fence to scrap their broken lawnmower."

Kevin sat up quickly. "Poison ivy? Was it terrible?" he asked.

"Are you sorry?"

Kevin nodded.

"Well, poison ivy... " And I launched into my subject.

The last Friday in August was Ellen's eighth birthday. Kevin would be five in three weeks. I thought we should have a party.

"But I don't know enough children," Ellen complained. "And Kevin hasn't got *any* friends."

We were sitting around the table eating canned peaches out of the pink bowls.

"I don't like children," Kevin said thoughtfully. "I like firemen."

"Well, I know a lot of people we can invite," I said, thinking of all my drinking friends who had been so appalled at the idea of me raising children. They would do for some very nice presents. "Grown-ups give better presents anyway," I told Ellen.

All summer we'd had a shortage of playthings. Besides *Little Women*, Ellen owned a box of 48 broken Crayolas and all the yellow second-sheets her father could bring home. Kevin owned a carton full of wooden building blocks. There had been a red sponge rubber ball we bought at Woolworth's, but it had gone down the sewer on 109th Street, and recently their father had come home with a bag of 60 brown plastic soldiers, each only an inch high. They had spread like an infestation of ants: underfoot, beneath the furniture, in the bathtub, floating belly-up in the dishwater. Two had accidentally gotten baked, and one melted around the coils of Mrs. Shaeffer's hinge-sided 1940s toaster. I would be leaving Ellen and Kevin soon. I thought a birthday party would provide them with some toys.

The morning of the party was hot and cloudless. Heat floated up from the street and through the open window where Ellen and Kevin sat, cutting lace doilies out of folded yellow paper. I was stirring a bowl of cake frosting mix, dropping in red food coloring to turn it pink. We had stacked three plain angel-food rings from the supermarket, and I was planning to ice the entire, spongy structure to make it look home-baked. Ellen wanted pink frosting. Four quarts of pistachio ice cream were in Mrs. Shaeffer's refrigerator and their father would be serving lime Kool-Aid and discount gin to drink. I began beating the mix: instead of pale pink, it was turning decidedly lavender. I added a few drops of yellow. Ellen put down her doily. "It's turning orange."

"Let me see." Kevin stood on his chair.

"Sit down with those scissors," I ordered. I quickly added a few more drops of red – the mix was rather liquid now – and we watched it shade to bright watermelon.

Ellen looked at me doubtfully.

"It's beautiful," I told her.

The mixture was quite runny now, and since there was no powdered sugar, I quickly thickened it with a little buckwheat flour we found in Mrs. Shaeffer's cupboard, so it would be stiff enough to spread on the cake.

Ellen opened the door. She was hostess in an ironed, pink cotton dress and polished strap shoes. A homemade aluminum foil crown sat above her wet, neatly combed bangs. I waited slightly behind her, trying to hold back my smile at the sight of our guests, young men-about-town, who stood on the threshold, looking embarrassed behind big store-wrapped packages tied with pastel ribbon. A few had even brought a date. Ellen admitted all graciously, taking each young man by the hand and leading him down the hall into the living room. Dishes of jelly beans sat on all the small tables and three balloons floated over Battersea Bridge. Kevin raced about in a similar foil crown, over-excited, making passionate dashes at the pile of presents. We finally had to put them all on top of the upright piano.

Even though we had opened all the windows, it was still hot in the apartment. The young men sweated, shaking hands and introducing their dates. They sat uncomfortably in a circle and tried to make suitable conversation. Out in the kitchen, we could hear the crack of ice cube trays as the children's father fixed drinks.

While we waited, Ellen politely passed around the jelly beans, and Kevin, spotting the prettiest of the dates, a young woman in a white cotton summer dress, climbed into her lap. "I like ladies," he told her. "Do you have any diseases?"

I quickly tore up strips of paper for animal charades.

In the darkened dining room, the guests stood around the Shaeffers' table singing "Happy Birthday" rather ginnily. A circle of candlelight glowed on our tall stiff cake. Standing on a chair, his knees against the table edge, Kevin leaned over the cake. The tiny flames cast darting shadows on his tilted features, lighting the underside of his snub nose. Ellen stood beside him to help, her cheeks flushed pink as the vivid cake frosting.

"Now, Anne?" Kevin asked. "Can we blow at them now?"

"Now."

Kevin swooped forward, woofing, while Ellen's cheeks belled. The candles flickered wildly for seconds between drafts, then sputtered out. In the sudden, wax-scented dark, everyone cheered.

Even though the cake cracked like a plastered wall when we tried to cut it and proved inedible, the party was a huge success. It ended with the grown-ups singing old summer camp songs for the children, and, at nine-thirty, Ellen and Kevin went docilely to bed, worn out by their own good behavior. When they were asleep, we drank more discount gin, and someone wisely sent out for pizza.

In the fall, the Shaeffers came home, and Ellen, Kevin, and their father moved into a new apartment one block up the street. Ellen started third grade at P.S. 125, while Kevin was sent to a neighborhood Episcopal school that had a kindergarten play group which lasted until five o'clock. I went back to Columbia. Our separate lives began.

It was the mid-60s before I got to Europe. Although World War II had ended there almost two decades earlier, austerity still gripped its edges. The dollar was strong. I was divorced and had finished grad school. With my long hair in braids for the photo, I picked up a Youth Hostel Card and didn't look back – going from London, to Brussels, Holland, Scandinavia, and finally, Italy, for just a few dollars a day. When the money ran out, I returned to New York. But as every writer who has tried to describe the sky over Umbria knows, you never really leave. My friend Susan, after an academic year abroad, had found a job in Rome. Which is why I began writing a book about our expeditions. To be titled – what else? – Innocent Broads. Only three chapters were completed.

ROTTING SAINTS AND VIRGIN MARTYRS

I LEFT ROME THAT JUNE knowing three hundred words in Italian, mainly names of things to eat, mostly flavors of the gelato I had discovered in Trastevere. Finding those gelatorias one hot afternoon had shown me the possibility of a vocabulary: I stared at the rows of icy sherbet behind frosted glass, read the names, and for 800 lire a scoop, acquired noun after noun. There was a gelato war in progress that year as local entrepreneurs strove to outdo each other. When traditional fruit flavors were exhausted, they invaded the vegetable realm: pomodoro, zucchina, melanzana. They sweetened rice, whipped regional cheese into dulcet "fior di latte," and eventually overreached themselves with a piselli green mixture that tasted canned.

In southern Italy, food and landscape seem to merge; the countryside reaches vine-like into the teeming cities. Rome is no exception. Each day fresh vegetables arrive in the Campo dei Fiore; bread emerges hot out of local ovens; ripe olives are tumbled into barrels; cheeses and hams revolve slowly on ropes, fuming the hot air of shops unsanitized by air conditioning. And cats hang out all over town waiting for something to drop.

Most mornings I rose early because Susan taught school. We drank our coffee at the local bar, and I was across the Ponte Sisto by seven to watch the city gear up.

Since the museums were closed at that hour, I began exploring Rome's old churches, which were open early for mass. Sometimes I visited as many as three in a morning, skirting the small band of worshippers; staring upward at the bare feet of angels soaring on baroque ceilings; systematically searching the chapel aisles for a Caravaggio or Domenichino. Side altars were often dark except for a rack of flickering vigil candles. With luck there might be a metered box where one could drop a 100 lire piece to briefly light some shadowed painting. While the faithful took communion in the nave, I was off behind pillars, dropping coins into echoing metal light boxes. Many great paintings were so wreathed in shadow that I wondered how anyone had ever seen them before.

By contrast, the miraculous statues or wonder-working icons were brightly lit. Supplicants kept candles burning. Sometimes festooning the niche of a beneficent Virgin, or an especially courteous local saint, were dozens of small silvery hearts with flames. They lined the walls like painful valentines, reflecting back the flickering candles. In some churches these offerings were encased by glass, and among those hanging hearts swung arms or legs, a foot, a silver hand, or a swaddled silver child. Once from behind a statue I saw a pair of tarnished eyes look back at me – and once a torso with an argent liver.

When the faithful left for work I was often alone, shivering on some far aisle, exploring chapels where entombed below the altar, a full-length saint lay silently rotting behind glass, its face covered by a gilt mask. A lapsed Catholic, I stared at these childhood legends, intrigued and filled with horror. Despite the rising heat of the day, the churches remained cold. When the chill became too great, I found a bar outside and drank a second cappuccino. The sunlight and heat, the tainted air and angry honking of small overheated cars quickly erased my thought that death was inevitably cold.

When the city shut down for the long mid-day meal, emptying the streets, I took my Italian wordbook up into the Janiculum and tried to memorize useful verbs.

Later, walking home along the pungent streets in Trastevere, I passed tables that appeared each evening along Via di San Francesco a Ripa. Where were they kept during the day? At dusk, like magic, Trastevere turned into an outdoor restaurant: each hidden square was a noisy banquet.

All day, I walked amid Italian sounds practicing the words I knew, frustrated when someone answered me in rapid local dialect. I addressed shopkeepers formally: "buon giorno" or "buona sera," depending. But once the greeting was out and I tried to buy wine or cheese, they began pressing the virtues of this vintage or that mozzarella: "È molto squisito, signorina. Molto delizioso." I smiled and pointed. I nodded and paid. I'd begun to feel as if I were walking through Italy encapsulated; a glass bell had been lowered and while life went on around me – conversations, signs, books, newspapers – I moved through a well-documented world with no idea of what was going on. When Susan got home at night, exhausted from a day of teaching, I talked too much.

One hot afternoon, I took a crowded bus out of the center through Via Nomentana to the Church of St. Agnes called "outside the walls." Agnes was one of the saints I'd been raised on and I wanted to see her church. At the convent school where I was sent at age eleven, our reading had been strictly monitored. While other girls made heroines of teen-age detectives, we were beached with the lives of the saints. St. Agnes, pictured with a lamb, was a popular volume – her martyrdom less terrible than St. Lawrence howling on his gridiron or St. Sebastian sieved by pagan arrows. For refusing to marry, Agnes had merely lost her head. She had only been thirteen, a virgin martyr, and the nuns held her up to us: Lamb of God.

It was nearly four when I reached Sant'Agnese Fuori le Mura and all Rome was headed back to work. My bus, going opposite, passed a stream of crowded cars. I stared out the window at enormous villas converted to pensione or schools, and clusters of modern food shops. I almost missed my stop because the route had grown suburban. The area looked too new and prosperous to conceal an ancient martyrdom.

I stepped off the bus in the afternoon sun and shielded my eyes. Heat radiated from the pavement – cement, not Roman stones – as I followed a sign pointing me down a paved street of modern buildings. The church grounds, hilly and overgrown behind wire playground fencing, opened onto a tarmac yard where some children were playing soccer not far from the entrance to a large basilica. I heard the sound of the ball thudding and their voices followed me inside.

The church interior was dark and cool after the Roman sun, and I halted to let my eyes adjust. Along the nave ran two tiers of columns with decorated arches, and high above the altar was a mosaic semi-dome. "Sixth century," my guidebook told me. A church had been built here over the "tomb of Agnes in 324 by the Christian emperor Constantine during the Christian peace." She had been dead a mere eight years then. Alive, she would have been twenty-one.

I walked toward the high dome, staring upward at the mosaic. On a field of gold, St. Agnes stood, enormous, hieratic, wearing a jeweled cope. She was flanked on either side by tonsured saints, while overhead the hand of God reached from a sky of pebble stars. Tall, crowned, and matronly, this was no Lamb of God. She had a simple comic face – a drawing of a face – sloe-eyed and Byzantine and pushing forty.

As I stood shivering beneath the dome, I discovered that I was not alone in the church. Voices echoed behind me and I turned to see a small group coming out of a doorway at the rear. I shut my guidebook and walked down the left aisle.

At its end was an ill-lighted sacristy and, seated by the door, a man was counting coins into a metal money box. He was short, gray-haired, and swarthy. Standing upright on the table by his hand was a big plastic flashlight. Inside two Italian girls and a tall blond boy were looking at the postcards for sale on a rack.

The man looked up as I entered and asked, "Catacombs?"

I had not thought to visit catacombs, although my book mentioned that some were preserved under this church. I'd avoided the big catacombs on the Appian Way, those tunneled cities of the dead that twist under Rome. This church was less visited, so I assumed the catacombs were smaller. He waited for my answer. I looked around and saw that the others were waiting for him.

"Perché non?" I said and handed him five hundred lire.

We began the descent single file, following him down a turning flight of stone steps, which became dark. The shapes of the girls in front of me were silhouetted by the old man's flashlight. We were underground where the walls on either side were brown and close. I brushed the cold dirt and shuddered. I hadn't known the earth would be so near and tight. The little man moved quickly and we scurried to keep close to the light. The silence seemed to muffle our footsteps and no one spoke.

At one turning the light ahead disappeared and, in panic, the tall boy bumped into me. We might still have gone back, but around the next corner the narrow tunnel intersected, fanning in several directions. I knew returning was impossible. There was a light here, a small faint bulb cabled to the dirt wall, and we could see the burial niches on either side, rising from ground to ceiling, row after row. I stared at those narrow shelves, which must have been close fits, and felt myself thrust into one and sealed here forever. My hand accidentally touched the wall and the brown earth crumbled under my fingers. I quickly shut my eyes and tried to remember the sunlight and the furious traffic sixteen centuries above our heads.

We moved deeper into the catacomb, and the cold tunnel darkened behind us. One of the girls whispered something to the other in Italian and the guide, hearing it, answered and laughed. His flashlight danced on the dirt walls. We stuck close together. It will end, I told myself. We came to another intersection and the guide shone his flashlight onto the wall. "Affossatore," he said to the girls. Then he looked at the boy and me. "Greevedigger."

Neither of us spoke.

"Greevedigger," he repeated. I looked at the ancient stone and saw the drawing of a figure with a shovel. "Greeeevedigger," he insisted.

I nodded quickly. "Grave digger," I said.

He seemed satisfied. "Tedesco," the tall boy announced. Our guide repeated the word in German and proudly said it for us in other languages. Then he smiled and motioned to us, indicating that he had a special treat. We followed him along another damp, narrow passage where he led us into a small crypt; the German boy had to stoop. There was a dim light just inside, and when we stood upright again we could see more rows of burial niches and, at one end, a big empty alcove that may have been the sepulcher of a martyr. Saint Agnes? But this was not his treat. Grinning, he motioned us closer. There was a grill in front of one burial niche and he shone his flashlight in.

The Italian girls drew back. One said something to the guide and he moved the light around inside. Invited to come closer, the boy bent to look and I saw his horrified face in the dancing light. He did not stay long. Our guide was enjoying himself.

It was my turn. He crooked his finger. I took the three obligatory steps and looked inside the narrow opening. The light shone on ancient bones, half sunk in earth, intact. The skull had rolled on its side and the open, earth-choked mouth cried out to me as if it were struggling to get up. I quickly stepped back.

We left the crypt in silence and followed the little man back along the narrow tunnel. It smelled of earth. There were no Christian paintings here or frescos of the saints. No good shepherd promising safe conduct. I knew that martyrdom was terrible, bloody, cold – and ended in the dark.

As we retraced our steps single file, I was last, following the dark shapes of our line and the bouncing light ahead, past endless rows of gaping burial niches. Empty now. As we wove silently through the tunnels – touching earth on either side – I grew leery of the dark welter of intersecting passageways behind us. I turned, thought I saw a shadow move, and hurried to keep up.

When we finally arrived back in the sacristy, no one lingered. We left our guide counting his tips, flashlight upright on the table, waiting for his next visitors.

Outside, the blinding sun was hot. I stood letting its rays warm me, relieved to escape the cold dark centuries below. Out on Via Nomentana, motorbikes and little cars fought noisily for space and the number 60 bus was full of passengers who didn't pay their fare. I rode that crowded bus standing, holding on tight and thinking about the catacombs under Rome as we swerved in and out of traffic. Outside, the Italian cars pressed on, horns blaring, the drivers shouting at each other, fists shaking. Very much alive.

That evening Susan and I ate supper beside her big open window looking out over TV aerials on seicento roofs. Music drifted up with the fumes from the restaurant below.

I poured more Rubesco into our glasses. I brought wine home each night from our enoteca, where they shelved the bottles by region. We'd worked our way from Friuli to Umbria.

"Questo vino è the best dei tutti we've bevere," I said.

"Bevuto," Susan corrected me. "Che abbiamo bevuto."

When I finally acquired enough words to handle both our local market and the Porta Portese, I set out for Naples.

EX VOTOS IN NAPLES

THE RAPIDO LEAVES ROME for Naples every hour during the day, and though the trip takes less than three hours, I had a feeling that I was leaving civilization. I knew Rome. I was uncertain about Naples. Susan had repeatedly warned me to be careful, to carry nothing that could be snatched. In Rome I kept my wallet in my jeans. But for Naples, Susan insisted that I wear the money belt she had made, a cotton pouch on a ribbon under my clothes. After three years of teaching in Italy, she wore her handbag cross-strapped and held it tightly. The local thieves of Trastevere took their coffee in the bar adjacent to our building. The cobble street was lined with motorbikes. When we went out, she would look about narrow-eyed, certain that one of them had grabbed her best leather bag last year. I was carrying my passport in the money belt and a thick fold of lire because the rate had been good that day. There was a suspicious bulge over my appendix, which I hoped might be mistaken for a tumor. I shifted on the train seat and tugged my cotton shirt down over it. My three-hundred-word vocabulary suddenly seemed inadequate.

The first sight of the Tyrrhenian coast comes at Formia, an old fishing village now booming with construction. Looking out the train window, I saw espaliered fruit trees and the fields, newly tented in plastic, which were giving us a bumper crop of gelati flavors.

Not long after, the rushing landscape rose sharply outside the train window as distant hills thrust higher where the earth cast them up. Vesuvius is unmistakable from the train: an ominous black cone where low clouds hang like smoke. Watching it from the window, I felt an ancient threat.

From the Garibaldi station, I checked into a second-class hotel below Piazza Carità, near the post office. My room was tiny; the bath and toilets were far down the hall. All the other guests seemed to be Italian. Susan, who traveled on a teacher's salary, knew of it. I dropped my duffle bag on the bed and set off to see the harbor while it was still light.

That evening I walked from Santa Lucia toward Posillipo, following that broad sweep of bay that curves toward Ischia. Out in the water, fishermen in rowboats bobbed beyond the Castel dell'Ovo, dropping lines. The air was cool and smelled of fish. I leaned my elbows on the seawall, looking far out while dark-haired teenagers strolled past, fingers entwined, or lounged against the stones, unembarrassed and ardent. I passed a waterside shrine and docks of anchored craft for hire to Capri. Further on, small boys dove off a reef of sharp rocks into cold-looking water. I walked until the light began to fail and I had to turn back.

That night I slept wearing the money belt. It was made from one of Susan's old summer dresses that I remembered from college.

Very early in the morning, I took a bus to the Capodimonte Museum, that Napoleonic stronghold in its high park above the city, where I looked at paintings in near solitude until the school groups began to straggle in. As the heat of the day rose outside, I left that cool retreat, following a map, determined to make my way on foot. Unable to ask directions, I retraced my steps often. Finally I found a flight of broken and deserted stone stairs sharply descending the wooded incline. I stumbled down the steep pitched steps, conscious of being alone and far from help, looking over my shoulder to see if I were being followed. Once I thought I saw a shadow, but when I looked again, it was gone. I passed no one on the overgrown incline and emerged, far below, onto a noisy, very dirty Neapolitan street. Cars were pulled onto the sidewalks and laundry dripped from balconies, often forcing me into the traffic.

I'd watched Neapolitans plunge out into that roaring traffic, seen old women in black dresses hold up gnarled hands at speeding cars that screeched and braked to a halt. But once off the curb, my caution won out. I hesitated and the mezzogiorno traffic rushed past me, hurrying home. It was the noon hour, when Italy pulls down its shutters. As I walked along, shops closed and blinds were rolled down. Even the dogs got up and went inside.

I walked a long way in the sun, smelling the odor of cooking, stepping over debris, looking at my map. Once I stopped to buy a glass of acqua minerale in a hot bar and drank the cold fizzy water, standing in its doorway.

By late afternoon, I had wandered into Spacca-Napoli, the very oldest area, where I sat on some broad steps outside a food shop in the Piazza del Gesù Nuovo, reading my map. Dozing in the sun by my feet was a dusty brown mutt with his tail pointed toward the church. If Rome is full of cats, then Naples, far poorer, is a city of dogs. I'd seen all shapes and sizes. They sat outside shops, slept in the shade of churches, watched with interest as I ate, and took their passeggiata through the dilapidated streets, ignoring speeding vespas and little cars. A few wore muzzles, but most, like the citizen at my feet, roamed free.

Out in the center of the rubbish-strewn piazza young men were kicking a black and white soccer ball around the ornate marble sculpture. Across the square stood the cut stone façade of the fifteenth-century Chiesa del Gesù Nuovo, which would open at four.

I saw the ex votos first, gleaming silver, dangling on ribbons from the slender carved fingers where petitioners had looped them – then I saw the whole wall of reliquary busts. They rose in shadow on both sides of the chapel in breathtaking splendor. Each saint's head was carved and polychromed with the delicate, entirely individual features so lovingly bestowed on figures in Neapolitan Christmas crèches. Their hands were carefully wrought, reaching out in prayer, blessing, or supplication. Seventy Italian saints, boxed in rows, looked at me from facing walls. Some were mounted atop crystal caskets that held their clearly visible bones; others concealed their sad human remains. The bottom row of saints, within reach of the faithful, were festooned with silver ex votos. They dangled off the delicate fingers, turning in the light as if the donors had just left. I stood beneath the wall of saints, looking at the sweet wooden faces, able to read only a few unfamiliar names in the shadowed light. They rose atop their poor bones, serene as Christmas angels, amid the baroque riot of colored marble.

I left the Gesù, recrossing the hot trash-strewn square, dodging bikes and screaming school children, to arrive on the tight confines of Via Benedetto Croce. I hugged the walls of streets six feet across as cars drove through, and wandered down narrow medieval passages with as many as four layers of laundry dripping overhead. Hurrying people and roaring motorbikes blocked the turnings and car brakes screeched.

In open doorways abutting the old streets, men worked or families lived in one room. An old woman in bed looked out at me surrounded by her meager furnishings and the household dog sniffed exhaust. Further on I saw the entrance to a palace and nearby the doors of a Renaissance church "in restauro."

The tiny shops lining Benedetto Croce are where Neapolitan jewelers conduct their trade; windows on either narrow side were festooned with rings, gold chains, cameos, and silver bowls. In one I saw ex votos for sale – so this is where they came from! – new silver arms and legs, feet. There were miniature silver men with fedoras, women, children, hearts, lungs, and eyes, a smiling mouth above a goitered throat, and babies of all sizes. I peered in the windows nervously, conscious of my blond hair. Would looking in a jeweler's shop telegraph that I was carrying money? But the Neapolitans strode by, sharing the sweltering street with roaring scooters and cars hitting their brakes. In several shops I saw the swaddled infant, its soft silver face looking like the baby Jesus. It would be wonderful to hang on a Christmas tree.

Finally I found a shop with its doors open and went in hesitantly. An elderly man seemed to be the proprietor.

"Buona sera, signore." I usually got that right. "Uh, ex voto in your finestra." Or was that Latin? I smiled furiously. "Per favore."

"Si, capisco." He smiled, showing stained teeth, and pulled a box from under the counter full of shiny new ex votos, each carefully stacked by limb or organ, wrapped in tissue and rubber banded.

"Grazie," I said, deciding to ask the price of several; one shouldn't show too much desire.

The little shop was stifling.

"Quanto costa?" I asked, picking up a silver heart. It had scalloped edges like a valentine and there was no silver mark. I suspected it was very low grade.

He took the heart from my hand and set it on a pair of hanging scales, adjusting little weights. "Otto," he announced.

Eight thousand lire, less than five dollars.

"E piccolo bambino," I said. "Quanto costa, bambino?"

He fingered through the box, saying words I didn't understand.

I saw a stack of swaddled infants and pointed. "Questa. Questa."

He picked it up and slid a new infant from under the rubber band. Still talking rapidly to me, he placed it on the scale. The needle swung across as he added a weight. "Dieci." Ten thousand.

The silver was tinny and light. I couldn't tell if he was putting up the price, but experience taught me that I was an obvious mark. "Grazie, signore," I said. Then I went into the act I'd developed in Rome to indicate that I did not have enough money with me. It got me out of stores. "Non oggi," I said regretfully. Then brightened: "Domani, signore. Domani mattina." I backed out, promising "domani." This would give me a chance to check prices in the other shops.

I tried two more stores further down. In one, rather toney, I was shown the same silver infant by a young man who unhesitatingly said, "Trenta." Thirty thousand! No scale was consulted.

"Troppo," I replied firmly. Too much.

In the other shop, I saw scales and insisted that the infant be weighed.

"Si, signorina," the proprietress made a show of adjusting the weights. The needle inched. "Quindici" she announced. Fifteen? It was the identical infant.

"Grazie, signora," I said. "Non oggi. Domani."

Outside, I started back, then remembering I'd told the first shopkeeper I had no money, I stopped. Behind me a motorbike screeched and I leaped against the building. The rider shrugged and passed me. Everyone in Naples drove on their brakes.

Still hugging the wall, I consulted my map and found I was near

Via Duomo – the blood of St. Januarius. I could return tomorrow. In the next bar I stopped and ordered a cappuccino with new authority.

The following morning I went to the big pink archeological museum, which closes at two. Susan had said it held the mosaics and frescos excavated from Pompeii. Those galleries were more extensive than I'd imagined and I wandered all morning among the house walls of families buried alive. When the museum closed, forcing me out, the city was in full shutter. I walked down the heat-clogged streets, dazed with antiquity, thinking about 79 A.D. The eruption would have been visible to anyone in Naples. I thought of the people of Herculaneum rushing into the sea. Terrified. Helpless. And then, like hundreds of other Neapolitans who live on the edge, I stepped off into heavy traffic and crossed Via Pessina. It was not as brave a gesture as it might have been an hour earlier during the rush hour.

The local wine was called Gragnano and cost less than bottled orange drink. I had a big glass with a round and ropey olive pizza. The crowded pizzeria was full of locals, and the young men who shoveled pies on wooden slats into the hot domed oven laughed and shouted to them. I felt shy and conspicuous, but it was a busy place and paid me the courtesy of not noticing. Unlike Italy's museum cities that rely on visitors, Naples accepted strangers, then ignored them. The only guidebook was hopelessly out of date and the official map quite useless. Naples left me to my own devices.

My time was limited, and I did not go to Pompeii, Sorrento, or Capri. Instead, I faced inward to Spaccanapoli. I roamed its twisting, poor, and dangerous streets in agitation as if I were trying to wrest some secret from them, and I did not return for my ex voto until the morning of my last day.

I had only a few hours before hotel checkout and was searching for the shop. As I hurried down the crowded streets, still hugging walls to dodge little cars, I heard a rooster crowing, and when I passed the piazza of St. Dominic, I spied him down a narrow passage: a big white rooster with a fine red comb strutting in circles between parked cars, crowing furiously and splitting the air with his complaint. He was, like the Neapolitan dogs, alone and in confident possession of the street.

I followed him down a shadowed passageway, where I saw some heavy doors and a small sign marking the Sansevero Chapel. I had read about that chapel, but hadn't found it. The street was deserted and the doors looked locked, but when I pulled the iron handle, they heaved open. Just inside, behind dingy glass, sat an old man selling admissions. This was still a private chapel, although I was not sure who benefited. It had been built in the sixteenth century by the di Sangros as a family burial vault. Their palazzo was across the way. What I wanted to see were the statues by Sanmartino, who had sculpted marble into net and gauze. And, indeed, in the center of that elaborate, small, baroque, and tomb-lined room lay his Christ, dead under a marble veil, features shining through the selfsame stone. A technique perfected; a curiosity; a tricky job of paring that had intrigued some eighteenth-century di Sangro.

The family tombs circling the walls were marble sepulchers of an earlier period, which I thought typical until I read that three held di Sangro nephews, all murdered on the same afternoon.

Off the main chapel a door opened onto a deep rotunda, where I heard voices coming up the stairs. A young Italian couple appeared, the girl talking so rapidly that she didn't see me when I smiled. I walked to the doorway of the rotunda, where stairs circled to a lighted floor not far below.

I did not see them until I was halfway down and then I stopped in horror, clutching the narrow rail. I had known; the book had mentioned it. But not this! A later di Sangro, a religious scoffer, had dabbled in the science of his day. His experiments were highhanded even for nobility. He had devised a formula, still unknown, that would solidify human veins and capillaries. And he used his science despite the cautious church. Proof lay here in his private burial vault.

Two gray and veinous bodies stood upright in glass cases, dead 300 years but held together by the intricate network of their hardened veins. The human circulatory system. Male and female: their hard-veined eyes looked out of decayed sunken flesh, and were pitiable. And no one knew who they were. Or how they died. Death was a quick and unremarkable thing in Naples then. This later di Sangro had prolonged it for us.

I left that strange necropolis without even looking back at the Sanmartino.

When the door shut behind me I was out in the dark cobbled streets once more and the rooster was gone. From the plain façade abutting the street, no one would guess what lay inside the chapel. I knew. And I recognized the shadow that had been following me since Rome. Nothing in the world – not all its good or splendor – could save me either. Everyone here knew that from birth, and the dark volcano looked down on them like destiny.

I returned to narrow Via Benedetto Croce with its cacophony and human traffic. Some thin adolescent boys followed me for a bit, but I carried nothing worthwhile.

I was looking for a bar to get some strong espresso when I saw the shop where I'd found my ex voto. I quickly crossed between cars and went inside. It was the right shop but the proprietor was not there. Instead, a gray-haired woman in a cotton dress was behind the counter.

"Buon giorno, signora," I began. "Dov'è votre marito?" It sounded foolish since I couldn't explain why I wanted her husband.

She answered something I did not understand.

I nodded as if I did, and pointed to the counter where I knew he kept the box of ex votos. "Per favore. Ex voto. Bambino per dieci. Votre marito, uh, told me, dieci."

She looked at me suspiciously, but brought out the cardboard box. I saw my ex voto on top.

"Questa," I said happily and reached under my jeans for my money belt, too pleased to be embarrassed. I fumbled with the pouch and extracted a ten thousand lire note, which I gave to her with some change.

Just as I handed across the lire, a very pregnant young woman in a smock hurried in, grabbed the note from the woman's fingers, and left the shop.

I turned, completely astonished – thievery? – and looked at the proprietress.

She burst out laughing. "Mia figlia, mia figlia."

"Oh," I said, relieved. It was her daughter. But so pregnant. I picked up the little silver infant. "Questa ex voto facit." I said. "It works."

She laughed. She held her sides. She had to sit down.

I smiled uncertainly and then laughed too.

"Carmella!" she shouted. "Carmella, vieni!"

The young woman in the smock came lumbering back. The story was told rapidly with many gestures. Carmella laughed. She rocked back against the counter and howled and clutched her extended stomach as if her hour had come.

I was startled, but kept smiling.

Carmella grabbed my hand and placed it over her ample heaving belly. "Grasso," she said. "Bambino grasso." She laughed and pressed my hand into the bouncing swell.

Suddenly her mother ran outside calling to the woman in the next shop, who arrived on the scene with her husband. The story was repeated with many gestures for their benefit and they too were convulsed. I couldn't understand a word except "bambino," so I smiled warily.

Soon everyone left, wiping their eyes, smiling at me, and pressing my arm as if I were a backward child who'd finally done something right.

The proprietress, still weak from laughter, mopped her face and picked up the silver infant to wrap it in tissue. She stopped, holding it up, and pointed at my left hand resting on the counter. "È sposata?"

I shook my head. "No." I wasn't married.

She looked at the silver ex voto and then back at me with a knowing nod, almost a leer. We were both women of the world.

Oh my God, I thought, accepting the wrapped package. I should have bought one of those silver men with the fedoras first.

"Grazie, signora," I said. "Grazie mille. Buon giorno, and, uh, arrivederci."

I stepped out into the sunlight on Via Benedetto Croce and walked right in front of a Fiat. I stood firm, shot up my hand, and he braked. Hah! I smiled at the car as I crossed Benedetto Croce heading for the real test that would come on Via Roma. Naples was dealing with a seasoned woman of the world who could make jokes in Italian.

GETTING TO PRIENE

EVERYONE IN TURKEY HAS A COUSIN who drives a dolmus, or so it had begun to seem to us. If it were not for these pervasive relationships, we might have taken a bus from Selcuk to see the ruins of Priene as our guidebook advised. However, from the day we arrived in Turkey, we'd been enriching cousins, uncles, brothers-by-marriage, and many other complicated strata of kinship. That none of these people bore the least family resemblance didn't seem to matter, and it was considered rude to notice.

So we should have been suspicious of the helpful young man who told us in halting English, sadly shaking his head, that we'd just missed the big bus to Soke and all the great archeological sites at Miletus, Didyma, and Priene. But, wait, he said, suddenly beaming, his cousin, who had a dolmus, was getting ready to make the run to Kusadasi – a mere ten minutes from Priene. In Kusadasi we could easily get another dolmus straight to the ruins: What a piece of luck! He indicated that we were just in time and I began to doubt.

Transportation in Turkey is largely free enterprise. There are many bus companies, all serving the most popular towns or sites. Each line has its ticket office with a squad of local youths who hawk, persuade, and intercept travelers. In addition to scheduled buses are dolmuses, small owner-driven vans or mini-buses with hand-lettered destinations posted above their dashboards. They drive predetermined routes, with passengers paying for whatever portion of the journey they rode. Susan and I had watched Istanbul Turks jam themselves into dolmuses. We'd seen scarved women and men in business suits hail battered vans, prise open the doors, and pile atop fifteen other passengers occupying twelve seats. Finally, we found the courage to wedge ourselves in alongside them. Sometimes dolmuses were the only way to get to a destination or a site. But they were rarely comfortable.

Susan looked at me. I shrugged; the point was to get there. We followed the youth to a gray van that was revving its motor. Eight Turks, all men, shifted to make room for Susan and me. Most were smoking. I ducked in saying "Merhaba" ("hello"), one of my three Turkish words. The cigarette smoke was thick. Susan shoved in beside me. Our driver hit the gas, the van lurched forward, we slammed against the seat front and were off. As we shot out of the Selcuk station, a bus pulled in. It was clearly marked: Soke. Susan and I looked at each other. Again!

Our dolmus was moving fast now. We turned off the main highway and raced toward the seacoast. The road was paved but grew steep and narrow as we pushed through dense forests of pine trees. The little van swayed, throwing us back and forth. I looked out the nearest window and straight over a precipice. The van shuddered, pulling against gravity.

"Can you reach the window?" Susan whispered. "I can't breathe."

I shook my head; I didn't know the word for window.

Susan groaned. We had discovered on the plane to Istanbul that Turks smoke anywhere and all the time. I prayed the thick fumes would not overcome our driver.

We'd reached the summit and one of the men pointed for us to look. Susan and I stared out at the distant Aegean, dark green and shining toward Greece. The view from Homer's time. Then we were hurtling downhill – would the brakes work? A man leading a donkey shot past us and disappeared. We clutched the seat, bracing as the road forked; everyone slammed right and the van slowed. I looked out and saw the first hotel, a cement and glass structure behind the trees. Abruptly we lurched off the road, came to a stop, and our Turkish friends climbed out. Susan looked at me; we'd just caught on. We had taken the daily workmen's van that delivered waiters, porters, and cleaners to the big resort hotels that rim the breathtaking shores of Kusadasi. Between hotel stops, we glimpsed sea and sand. Beach umbrellas unfurled in the early sun and a huge ferry steamed out toward the nearest Greek island.

When we finally reached town, our dolmus was empty. Susan counted out the exact amount she'd seen the Turks hand over. "Gunaydin" ("good day"), we told the driver, and he sped away, leaving us staring into traffic. It was already nine and the sun was hot on our uncovered heads.

"Priene?" Susan kept asking Turks, who smiled accommodatingly.

Suddenly I spied a van with PRIENE hand-lettered in its window. I shouted and Susan waved her jacket; the dolmus veered sharply through oncoming traffic, toward us. It was painted a pale blue and there were five young Turks in the back seats. As we scrambled aboard the driver turned around.

"Priene?" we said.

"Priene," he replied with a knowing grin. In back, all five Turks smiled invitingly. The door slammed, gears screamed, the van jolted – it was too late – we were off. I landed beside Susan on the middle seat: springs covered with an old kilim. Outside, the paint was new, but inside was a harrowing muddle of wire. He must have rehabbed a wreck. As we sped away, I heard Susan swallow. I quickly searched for road signs and checked our map; we were headed in the right direction. Suddenly the van wheeled 90 degrees toward the other curb, where a prosperous-looking man in shirtsleeves opened the front door and jumped in beside our driver – he seemed to know it was the only intact seat. He greeted the other men, turned to show us a magnificent mustache, and spoke in rapid Turkish to our driver. I did not understand, but would have sworn that they were bargaining. Our driver shook his head; the passenger disavowed it; our driver released the steering wheel to point at us; the van swerved; the passenger upped his offer. I looked at Susan. The dolmus drove this route daily; what could happen?

In minutes we knew. As we entered the next town, Soke, our dolmus veered sharply and turned onto a side street where we rumbled along a narrow sunless passage, braked suddenly, and backed into a dark garage with lots of men standing around. They seemed to be expecting us. Susan zipped her jacket and I fingered my Swiss army knife.

Our driver cut the engine and our Turks opened the rear doors and jumped out. Then, as Susan and I watched, they all began hoisting, lifting, staggering under the weight of enormous sealed paper bags; loading them into the back of our dolmus. Cement! The van dipped and groaned as bag after bag landed on the platform behind the rear seats. When it was dangerously low, they slammed those doors and piled more bags between the seats. Finally our Turks got back in, putting their feet on the bags, while the driver and his friend jumped in front. As the dolmus started up, the driver turned to Susan and me and said something apologetic in Turkish. The van jerked its load forward, the rear tires shuddered, and we were off once more to Priene.

As we left Soke, our driver and the prosperous Turk were talking so rapidly that we sped past a man jumping up and down in the road and waving his arms. Our driver hit his brakes; we grabbed the seat backs; cement shifted behind us, and the van rocked to a fast stop. As we backed up, the man hurried toward us. He seemed to be dragging or rolling an object that was round and black: a huge metal sphere the size of a beach ball with steering wheels on both ends!

"Oh no," Susan said. "He's got a bombola. That's what it's called in Italy; a drum of cooking gas. They use them up in the hills."

The Turk with the bombola opened our side door, greeted the driver, and faced three bags of cement. Undaunted, he climbed atop the bags, pulled the enormous canister up into his arms, and managed to shut the door.

"Can it explode?" I whispered. Susan didn't know.

We lumbered off down the road, rocking and shaking: a baby blue grenade. Traffic beyond Soke was providentially sparse.

We'd covered five miles when our driver suddenly turned off the highway onto a dirt road that wasn't even on the map. We followed this stony road as it twisted upward through the trees. The grade was almost vertical. Our gear stick shuddered as the driver wrestled it into second. His tires gripped, stone by stone, up the incline. He shouldn't have been able to do it. We held on tight and everybody leaned forward. Cement thudded against the rear doors.

Up ahead we could see a village of old stone houses where small children and dogs were watching us. Chickens scurried out of our way. Suddenly the Turk with the bombola shouted and our driver pulled hard on the hand brake. The Turk quickly handed across some lire, opened the door, and, still clutching his gas canister, jumped off three bags of cement. As the door slammed, we saw him rolling his lethal sphere toward his house.

Our driver released the brake and we slithered backwards on loose dirt, then began lurching upward once more. The mustachioed passenger was pointing toward a high settlement of very old stone houses, where we could see men working. We lumbered upward until the road ended suddenly. Our driver braked fast, grinding gears, and backed onto a siding. The Turks immediately jumped out of the van, and one located a large rock to wedge under a front wheel. This was a trick we'd seen in Istanbul with its perilously steep streets. Drivers often left rocks curbside for each other.

There was a fall of pebbles as the workmen came down to greet us; then everyone formed a chain to pass bags of cement out of our van and up the vertical footpath. Susan and I watched as new Turks stared in at us. The sun overhead was rising fast toward noon and it was getting hotter. Some dogs wandered over to smell our tires and a small curious goat watched from high ground. The old houses, even lacking roofs, were handsome in the strong light and I was cheered that they were being repaired.

Finally the last 100 pounds left the dolmus and our Turks climbed back in, leaving their mustachioed friend with his cement. As our driver got in, he gave Susan and me a sheepish grin – business is business – and turned the ignition.

"The rock!" I said to Susan. "Stop!" I shouted and pounded his seat. "Hayir!" ("No!") – a rock… under your wheel!"

"Basta!" Susan yelled in Italian.

Our driver turned and stared at us as if we'd gone mad. Women! Americans!

We waved our arms and pointed. Suddenly a young Turk remembered and called out something. Light broke across our driver's face: Understanding. Embarrassment. Chagrin. While the boy dashed around to remove the rock, all the Turks began talking and nodding at us. We didn't understand a word, but clearly we had scored for the distaff.

As we bumped down the steep incline with alarming speed, our driver kept turning around to express his gratitude. Susan and I returned his smiles through clenched teeth.

Fifteen minutes later, we finally reached the archeological site. All the Turkish passengers had left; the sun was high, and we were hot, thirsty, and grooved from springs under the kilim. Nevertheless, our still-grateful driver insisted on showing us around the small tourist area before he'd let us out of the dolmus. We saw a modern restaurant, a smaller teahouse, and shops full of ubiquitous alabaster souvenirs. Our driver shook his head to warn us that these establishments were over-priced. Then he dropped us near a canteen with six outdoor tables. We understood immediately. This restaurant belonged to his relative (and he got a percent if he brought in trade).

We handed over our fare, promising to return there for lunch. I couldn't wait to see the back of that dangerous and stifling van. The 25 miles from Selcuk to Priene had consumed two hours already. We said goodbye and waited to make sure he drove off.

Susan and I climbed the steep road to the archeological site in bright Aegean sunlight. The route was solitary and fringed with high grasses and weeds, but when we reached the shelf of Mt. Mycale, Priene was waiting. High, wild, and splendid, it had undergone none of the heavy restoration that Turkey's more famous sites had suffered. Priene lay much as it had fallen two thousand years before. Standing in noon sun under a blue sky, we studied our site map. It had become unseasonably hot. I rolled up my sleeves and Susan tied the arms of her jacket around her waist. Butterflies floated above the high weeds and lighted on fallen stones. We began walking; checking our guidebook with its re-created city plan. Priene was a small town – we could see that from its ruins. Our book said "never more than four thousand citizens."

Susan looked at the plan. "We should be near the Agora," she said. "But I can't be sure."

We went on. Priene's streets are tiered and it lies on many levels. Alexander the Great stopped here in 334 B.C., I read, and erected a temple dedicated to Athena. We had a temple to find.

I pushed my sunglasses up on my perspiring nose and looked at the diagram: "We're bound to be near the temple... if we're here," I looked doubtfully at the piled stones. "Are we here?" It took practice to find the outlines of archaic buildings. Two fluted cylinders from fallen columns stood shoulder high beside us on the overgrown path where an ancient wall held back the surge of nature. Nature was prevailing.

We found the Temple of Athena on the next level: five tall pleated columns with Ionic capitals stood re-erected on what remained of its foundation. Steps led up to these solitary pillars, which rose white against the gray mountain face. Priene's Athenaeum was a model of classical temple construction in its time, and much copied. Susan and I took pictures of each other standing beside those stately columns – not for vanity, but as a way to indicate height. The temple had been surrounded by columns, we read, which explained all those fluted drums fallen on the walks below.

We wandered up narrow streets in blazing sun under a brilliant sky, trying to imagine the little town. Its buildings had been small. Even Priene's theater was diminutive compared with the acrophobic heights and span of the great ancient theaters. Priene's tiny, overgrown semi-circle was intimate. Twelve rows had been excavated. Spaced around the lowest seats were five stone armchairs with fingered hands and carved lion feet – for dignitaries. In the glaring light some young Germans, a woman and two men, were taking photos of each other sitting in those chairs. They wore khaki shorts and good hiking boots. Susan and I waited for them to leave before we sat in the chairs and took our own photos – to illustrate comparative size, of course.

Many ruins later, we spied the Germans climbing up the precipitous hillside to reach some higher monument. We tried to follow, scaling that rocky slope in the hot sun, and discovered what dangerous places real archeological sites are.

"If I break a leg," Susan said, scrabbling for a handhold on some bushes above me, "who do we call?"

I dug my fingernails into the steep hillside, watching pebbles slide past me.

"This may not be the best idea we ever had."

"I'm starving," Susan said.

Leaving danger to the better-equipped Germans, we retraced our steps through ruined Priene, back to the main entry road. The sun, still high, had begun to slant past lunch. Trying not to hurry, we walked back down the steep road to the area of shops and restaurants.

Susan decided that our driver's cafe was "more authentic" than the modern restaurant, and chose it, although we were the only customers. We ordered bottled water to drink under a saggy green awning, and ate a typical, unchanging Turkish meal: crumbly white cheeses, salads of finely chopped tomatoes and cucumbers with mint, hummus, kebabs, fresh bread. The food was cool in our mouths and the oil was good. Delicious and cheap. We were almost willing to forgive our driver for that dangerous uncomfortable trip.

I was dipping my second chunk of bread into hummus when Susan choked and grabbed her napkin. She coughed frantically and pointed.

I spun around to see a pale blue van turn into the open square bus park. It circled the area slowly until the driver spotted us and accelerated. The blue dolmus pulled right up alongside our table, shaking the green awning. Our driver leaned far out of his window, grinning familiarly at us: "Merhaba! Merhaba!" We were in luck, he indicated cheerfully. He had returned for Susan and me, his good friends, and was waiting to drive us back – even all the way to Selcuk.

Looking through my early files of great titles, promising openings, and half-written novels going nowhere, I wonder why I never wanted to write anything but fiction. But I kept trying, collecting rejection slips, working in libraries to pay my rent, and taking subways. It was a time in New York City when Boy Scouts were beginning competitive "subway marathons" – riding the entire system on one token in the least amount of time. One night in the early '70s a friend who wrote for the Daily News *asked if I had any new ideas for their* Sunday News *magazine. I said, "What about the marathons? No woman has done a subway marathon." He asked, "Could you do it?" I thought I could and began my journalism career.*

AROUND THE TOWN IN 26 HOURS AND 36 MINUTES

THE LEFFERTS BLVD. STATION at four in the morning could be the loneliest place in New York. Or maybe just the coldest. Wind blows across the elevated tracks. I look out of the train – suspended here – waiting for the return runs to Manhattan. Outside the night is dark except for some metal lamps on the deserted platform. Bare light bulbs form little circles of heat in the cold air. I am absolutely alone. Reflected in the train windows are its baby-blue walls splashed magenta and orange with graffiti. Beyond them I can see the black tops of trees, the low buildings of Queens stretching west toward Brooklyn. Far off, a yellow glow indicates Manhattan. Shivering, I cross to the open door and step out onto the platform. It is very still. A quarter moon hangs over Ozone Park, where all sensible people are asleep.

It might be warmer below near the token booth. Perhaps there is even a candy machine. But if the train should suddenly pull away...? No, I decide. Even if there is a machine, it won't be working. There are some 6,600 vending machines in the New York Subway System. I know of four that work. The Interborough News Co. owes me eighty-five cents. *Dear Sirs...* I begin composing a letter in my head – then stop. If I give the locations of all the stations where I lost coins yesterday, they'll think I'm mad. Some of those stations are 50 miles apart!

It seems to me that I have been here an eternity. I look at my watch: 20 minutes. This wait could ruin my chance at the world record. It stands at 21 hours and 8 minutes.

The first subway riding record – traveling the entire system of routes for a single fare – was set October 27, 1904: IRT Opening Day. The subway, a historic 9.1 miles, extended from City Hall to Grand Central, turning west across 42nd St. to Times Square, and then up Broadway to 145th St. After an official opening trip by city dignitaries – with Mayor McClellan holding a silver controller – followed by several hours of invitational rides, the subway was opened to the public at 7 p.m. 111,881 passengers paid a nickel each to ride that day. Scheduled time for an express was 26 minutes; the local took 46. Although those early riders were conscious of making history, it is doubtful that they had any thoughts of setting track records. It was just too simple.

The new subway generated appendages almost yearly. It reached Brooklyn via tunnel in 1908. The success of the IRT encouraged more construction. The Brooklyn Rapid Transit (after 1923, the BMT) began operations in August 1913, and the city-operated IND was opened September 10, 1932. Under the dual contracts by which the city had financed construction of the privately operated IRT and BMT, it had also retained the right to purchase them. In 1940 both were acquired for $326,248,000. The three lines were unified under city control on June 12 of that year.

Two days before unification, Herman Rinke, a curious and still indefatigable electric railroad enthusiast, decided to tour the existing system for a single five-cent fare. He had no thought of setting a record. With unification, the IRT-operated Ninth Ave. El was scheduled for demolition. His trip was a 25-hour sentimental gesture. It turned out to be the first recorded try. Since that day, 66 people have ridden the entire system in 24 recorded trips. These records are kept in an unofficial file at the TA Public Relations Dept. No one knows how may kids have done it just for fun. The 1961 subway map cited the example of a Flushing youth who had ridden all the routes in 25 hours and 36 minutes *for a single token*. The TA's aim may have been to point out the scope or convenience of the subway, but that record – set January 25, 1957, by Jerome Moses, 16 – instead seemed to invite competition. During the 1960s, subway derbies became a fad with urban students; 11 of them were completed during the peak years of 1966 and 1967. On April Fools' Day of 1966, the M.I.T. Rapid Transit Club began a highly publicized ride. They had used a computer to route their attempt and informed the newspapers. On April 2, they were feeling foolish by 1 hour and 1 minute. And Geoffrey Arnold, who had held the 24 hour, 56 minute record since 1963 when he was 17, remarked, "Pacific St. was a ridiculous place to start." That June, nine Boy Scouts from Troop 290 in Queens further shamed the computer by logging 23 hours and 18 minutes. And on August 3, 1967, 16-year-old James Law, with six buddies, rode from 168th St., Jamaica to Pelham Bay Park in 22 hours 11½ minutes; a time cited in the current *Guinness Book of World Records*.

When the Bronx Third Ave. El was closed in August 1973, subway route mileage was diminished 5.5 miles. On October 8, Mayer Wiesen, 35, and Charles Emerson set a "modern record," riding over 230.8 route miles, changing trains many times, and passing through the 462 operating stations, in 21 hours and 8 minutes – a record that looks as if it will stand unless I get out of the Lefferts Blvd. Station.

At 8 yesterday morning, I am just starting out, entering the 168th St. terminus of the Jamaica spur, an old elevated line taken over and extended by the BMT. The 1893 span between Alabama Ave. and Cypress Hills may be the oldest el track still in continuous use. The train I board is one of the oldest also: rolling stock built in the mid-1930s. Sixty-watt bulbs light the cars. Hanging down from the ceiling are fans with black blades. I make my way to the front car, intending to ride looking out the window next to the motorman's cab, but a handsome black kid, about 13, has gotten there first. He stands, hands in his pockets, nose to the glass, alert, ready to "drive the train." At 8:03 we head toward Manhattan – looking down long streets of old houses, over expressways clogged with morning traffic, rattling past Cypress Hills Cemetery where miles of tombstones cast small, neat shadows in the early light. At Broadway-Myrtle, I change to the M train, yoyo-ing up and back to cover the Myrtle Line – past houses whose third-story windows, with pulled blinds, are often no more than six feet from the train.

9:15. Manhattan comes into view from the Williamsburg Bridge. The huge building blocks that pile its shore jut powerfully at the sky.

Below, the East River is gray. It is a postcard approach. The train "zooms-in" like a 1940s movie – so familiar that I almost expect to see titles flash across. No matter. The Manhattan skyline still makes me gasp.

10:00. I am changing trains in Brooklyn when I see the kid from the Jamaica el again. We grin in recognition. "Hey," I shout, "Are you doing the system too?" As the train doors shut, I see him nod. He swings off to Coney Island, while I race up in search of the Astoria train. On the DeKalb overpass I spot a snack bar and buy a Coke for breakfast. Aside from some coins in my jeans, a notebook and map, I have decided not to carry anything – sort of an urban Camp Fire Girl.

11:12. En route to Flushing on a blue World's Fair train. To my left Shea Stadium passes; while off to the right lies Flushing Meadow. The ribbed Unisphere and skeletal towers of the '64 Fair rear up out of the flat landscape – fossilized like dinosaurs.

12:05. Returning to Manhattan, I change at Jackson Heights for the newer IND. On the underpass is a Nedick's – coffee and a hot dog – breakfast is shaping up. I am wiping mustard off my fingers when I reach the underground Roosevelt Ave. platform. On May 2, 1970, this was the site of the first subway fatality due to collision or derailment in 42 years; two GG trains collided during evening rush hour, killing two passengers and injuring 71.

1:55. The F train to Coney Island is one of the new, longer R-44 models: pristine and elegant, with seats of muted orange and yellow. Panels of fake wood are set into its walls and fluorescent lights line the ceiling. Just before the doors close, a chime sounds – rather like the Avon doorbell. The advertising cards, color transparencies lit from behind, glow. These are the poshest cars to travel the subways since No. 3344, "The Mineola," rolled through in 1904. No. 3344 was the private coach of financier and IRT organizer August Belmont. His car had *real* wood, mahogany, with velvet-draped picture windows so that guests could enjoy the flashing signals while white-coated stewards broiled steaks in the galley and served iced champagne. Above them, Empire ceilings arched, pale green and gilt; the washroom windows were stained glass. If one cares to make a comparison, the Mineola can be found in the Branford Trolley Museum at East Haven, Connecticut.

I am about to succumb to the quiet style of these long, air-conditioned cars when I notice that the doors between them are kept locked. Existing subway tunnels were built for 60-foot cars, more the size, if not the décor, of the Mineola. These new, 75-foot units do not mesh properly on curves; the space between cars becomes dangerous. Motormen, conductors, and presumably transit police have keys, but New Yorkers are naturally leery. Many feel that being trapped in one car could become a risky situation.

The IND Coney Island line becomes elevated for a brief span entering Brooklyn; the highest point in the system, 87.5 feet above street level, is at the Smith and Ninth St. Station. Here the view is open in all directions: back toward postcard Manhattan, out into the harbor. Little automobiles crawl over the arched expressway ahead; below lie the Gowanus Canal and Red Hook. Too soon, we are underground.

At Church St. the line ramps upward again, joining the 1919 BMT el track at Ditmas Ave., where it emerges and begins the long approach to the ocean. Coney Island, cold and closed, decorates our passage. Orange and green spokes of the Wonder Wheel circle blue sky; flags and bits of banner blow. A deserted but honky-tonk air prevails. We pass the roller coaster, webbed and delicate in the afternoon light. The air is bracing.

2:54. The Brighton Line heads back to Manhattan, for a while paralleling the sea. Short views down streets end in ocean. The pastel acres of Brighton Beach Baths stretch, patterned, toward the sand. We stop at Sheepshead Bay before heading northwest, traveling over the old ground level tracks of the 1890s Brighton Railroad, widened in 1907 to cut through the tree-hung backyards of Victorian mansions facing Buckingham Road.

3:15. At the Prospect Park Station hundreds of high school kids mill, going home. Cops range the platform and one accompanies us onto the Franklin Shuttle. The kids are wonderfully natty; boys and girls stride aboard wearing platform shoes that defy balance, pants with big bells, hats, lots of jewelry, elaborate hair-dos. While I am aware that teenagers in groups are responsible for a fair amount of subway crime, I cannot imagine this stylish group doing anything to muss their clothes. Subway history is full of accounts of rampage and vandalism. Two days after the 1904 opening, eight youths armed with buckshot blowers boarded the new subway at 145th St. and proceeded to shoot out the electric lights while doing gymnastic stunts on the straps. Two were arrested at 96th St., the rest escaped. But this was not the first subway crime. *That* occurred opening night. During the crowded ride north from Brooklyn Bridge Station, someone lifted the $500 diamond stickpin that had been holding down the tie of Harry Barret of W. 46th St. When he reached Grand Central, his necktie was flapping.

3:50. The return shuttle is almost empty. As it approaches Prospect Park again, we pass near Empire Blvd. In November of 1918 it was still called Malbone St. The name was changed after the Brighton Beach Special, jammed with evening rush hour passengers, failed to make a curve at the tunnel there. Five wooden cars, taken over from the old Brooklyn Union Railroad, were dashed to bits, and passengers thrown rapidly along the tunnel walls literally had their faces rubbed away. Ninety-seven lost their lives, 150 were injured, and for days the accident drove World War I right off the front pages. When motorman Edward A. Luciano gave himself up, he was found to have had only two hours of instruction before being given the controller at Park Row in Manhattan. Earlier that morning – before motormen walked out in a dispute over unionization – Luciano had been a yard switchman. His promotion was sudden – this was his first run. He was acquitted, and the union made its point.

5:02. I am picking up a few stray miles under Rockefeller Center when evening rush hour begins. While I know the total 3.8 million daily subway riders cannot all be taking the D train tonight – it *feels* as if they are. Jammed shoulder to shoulder, passengers have nowhere to look but up. Above our heads, "Miss Subways" stares out of her poster, giving us a strained smile, "hoping to do some modeling." Since 1941, when the contest began, over 200 New York working girls have become "Miss Subways." In the early years, a new face showed up every month. Currently, two winners, out of six finalists, are chosen every eight months by passenger vote. Miss Subways receives a $40.00 charm bracelet dangling silver tokens, and her picture decorates the 6,700 subway cars for a three-month period. I ride standing all the way to 205th St., Bronx. Sheer endurance does not win a girl the title.

6:10. At 168th St. and Broadway, I change trains again, and descend into the IRT on a hot automated elevator to ride the Seventh Ave. local to Van Cortlandt Park. The ride is through the deepest section of track in the whole system: 180 feet below street level at the 191st St. and St. Nicholas Ave. station.

7:00. Moving under Harlem on the No. 3, a rather splashy train with big graffiti – mustard yellow and pink predominate. Despite

$10 million spent to remove graffiti and 1,562 arrests in 1972, the TA is losing the "spray can war." I read off the names – Supreme King 219, Snake II, Lopez 138 – and amuse myself trying to think up my own subway logo, in case graffiti should become legal. Outside the stations pass, dingy, written all over. Two Black Muslims move in and out of the strap-hangers selling *Mohammed Speaks*. On this line, I am a "token white" – the pun lifts my spirits.

8:02. TA police range the E. 180th St., Bronx platform where the No. 2 pauses. One boards, walkie-talkie mumbling at his waist. He will be riding until 4 a.m. Since May of 1965, a uniformed transit patrolman has been assigned to every train during these hours.

10:30. I stand in the first car, face pressed against the glass, speeding through a dark, underground world, the lighted coach behind me forgotten, as the black tunnel comes on. Tracks in perspective lines rush, disappearing under my feet, crossing, converging ahead. Signal lights change: yellow – "proceed with reduced speed," green over yellow – "on diverging track." Express lines mount, as local tracks sink in the dark. In the distance, tiny orange lights flicker above the tracks, then disappear where track-men carrying lanterns dive into the sidings. Now the square, metal-pillared cut rounds into a tube; we approach the old 1908 Battery-Joralemon tunnel. Green lights signal us through. I make myself useful peering intently at the dark curved walls, checking for leaks.

1:12. The Wilson Ave. station on the Canarsie line is a narrow, double-decked curiosity: one track occupies each level – the eastbound track emerges, briefly elevated, traveling above the underground westbound span. We pass the deserted platform in half light. It faces – a single track away – the Cemetery of the Evergreens. No one in his right mind would get off at Wilson Ave. at 1:12 in the morning. No one did.

2:30. The A train heads out over the waters of Jamaica Bay, leaving behind the huge glow of JFK that arc-lights the eastern sky. I have made the Rockaway Round Robin on schedule and can relax. Only between the hours of midnight and 6 a.m. is it possible to cover the entire Rockaway peninsula on a single train. This nineteenth-century summer beach resort was linked to the L.I.R.R. until 1956, when service was transferred to the IND. The train moves further out across the vast, dark bay. Only a few feet below on either side, water laps the narrow trestle. Far out, a crescent of lights veers gently inward on the long railroad stem. Beyond that brilliant curve, the ocean pounds. For miles around the night is black and cold, the water deep. A strange place for a New York subway train.

4:00. And farewell to Lefferts Blvd.

5:30. Waits are long now. The work trains move slowly underground through nearly empty stations, picking up trash and cleaning out tunnels. The New York bars have closed, and some standees on the Hoyt St. platform bear witness to this fact. A heavy woman joins me; she walks as if her feet hurt, and I suspect she has just gotten off work. The trains always take a while at this hour, she tells me. We stand together on the platform, unacknowledged sisters, re-enforcing each other. In 1907, the Hudson Tubes were still running Women Only Cars with guards aboard to insure protection. I guess we *have* come a long way.

At 6:26 the sun rises over Greenwood Cemetery where I am passing, for the second time, over an elderly bit of track known as the Culver Shuttle; 1.1 miles still bear tribute to Andrew Culver, who built a steam railroad to Coney Island that passed over this site in the 1880s.

7:00. Coney Island for the second time in two days! Crossing the Stillwell Terminal overpass, I go by the employees cafeteria and smell breakfast. On the Sea Beach Line, morning rush hour is just beginning. This is the third rush hour I have ridden through without leaving the subway. The poignancy of that situation might be enough to make one who has dined off Zagnut bars, peanuts, and Lucy Ellen orange slices for two days, get a cramp. I try not to think of hot coffee.

8:10. Changing trains at Union Square I am especially careful, warned by history. The first subway passenger accident occurred here on Opening Day, 1904. A Miss Sadie Lawson, 26, of Jersey City, who had been riding north and south for several hours, fell getting off the southbound train and broke her hip. I grab a metal strap and hang on tightly all the way to 42nd St.

8:25. Times Square. The 42nd St. shuttle contains 2,700 feet of original 1904 IRT track, now isolated. In 1928, the second-worst accident in New York subway history happened just south of here on the Seventh Ave. line. A defective switch broke as the ninth car of a 10-car theater rush-hour train was passing over it. The rear wheels switched to a diverging track and the ninth car, running suddenly at right angles to the others, was sheared in two by the steel pillars between tracks. This mechanical "crack the whip" killed 18 passengers and injured 100.

9:30. The Lexington Ave. Express emerges into bright sunlight just before the old Yankee Stadium. Once, under a glaring blue sky, its lacy wood trim gleamed white like decorative icing – a great hollow cake with a short right field. Now, under the ungentle touch of the renovators, the place is growing unrecognizable. At the Woodlawn terminus, the leaves have lost their fall colors, but on the golf course below, lucky men tee off across rolling fairways. It is a splendid day for riding elevated trains.

10:39. Pelham Bay Park. I have made the trip – on 67 different trains – in only 26 hours and 36 minutes. 26 hours and 36 minutes! The thought that I may be the first woman to complete the ride does not console me at all. But the sun is shining. And I have my graffiti logo: Ms. Subways 114.

For four years I worked as a "stringer," both proposing and being assigned stories for the New York Sunday News *magazine. The best were assignments that regular staff turned down, such as the Metropolitan Opera's new production of* Boris Godunov — *a three-hour work that I sat through 13 times, including one rehearsal of full orchestra with nothing but lighting cues. I even wrote a few short cooking pieces when the weekly food section needed fill.*

THE EDUCATION OF
A HOPELESS COOK

TONIGHT'S CLASS
Mousse au Caviar
Canard à l'Orange
Pommes Frites
Salade Verte
Poires à la Crème Anglaise

THE SIGN IN THE COOKING SCHOOL window made me hesitate. It sounded hard. And then I thought, "French cooking – that ought to impress my friends." So I went in.

The school turned out to be the lower floor of a converted East Side brownstone; its front section was a shop that sold gourmet utensils, the rear contained a model kitchen. I was the last student to arrive. Four women and three men were already seated on stools at a high counter behind which our instructor and her assistant were working. Before each student was a place setting of silver and a wine glass. Two very naked ducks lay on the counter. The French cooking course had been in session for several weeks, but it was not full and I had been allowed to join. Everyone looked at me as I climbed onto my stool. I smiled uncertainly. "Don't worry," the woman beside me whispered. "You'll love it. We have such *fun*!" I wondered what she meant.

As I watched, our instructor clipped both ducks' wingtips, performing a half-nelson to double the wings under, and began pulling out excess fat. ("How to truss a duck," I wrote in my notebook. "Make sure butcher has removed oil sacs in tail, put duck's legs through holes where sacs were, cross feet, tie. Fold neck flap down, skewer.") Now our instructor took a two-pronged fork and began furiously pricking both ducks' skins in the fat parts so grease would flow out as they roasted. (I wrote: "Purchase two-pronged fork. Secret of duck is *holes*.") Both trussed ducks were placed in a roasting pan on a rack astride a bed of vegetables for aroma: celery, carrots, potatoes. "If you don't use a rack," our instructor warned, "your duck will fry in its own grease." ("Buy roasting pan with rack," I wrote. "Do not let duck wallow.") The ducks disappeared into a wall oven at 450 degrees.

Thwack! I was nearly jarred off my stool. Thwack! Our instructor was chopping the necks and giblets with a huge cleaver. "Strong brown duck stock," she announced, tossing the giblets into oil to sauté before adding the remaining vegetables, a can of chicken broth, and a can of beef bouillon.

While our duck stock simmered, we would have time to make a caviar mousse. "Use cheap black caviar," we were told. "About two ounces." Her instructions went like this: Soften one tablespoon gelatin in one-quarter cup cold water for 10 minutes, place gelatin container in boiling water till gelatin is dissolved, and set aside. To caviar, add three hard-boiled eggs finely sieved ("Buy fine sieve."), one tablespoon coarsely grated onion, one teaspoon Worcestershire sauce, one-half cup mayonnaise, one clove garlic, pressed. ("Buy garlic press," I wrote. So far the only utensil that I seemed to own was the can-opener.) This mixture, folded into the gelatin with a teaspoon of lemon juice, was poured into a greased, decorative metal mold. ("Secret of French cooking is fully equipped French kitchen," I wrote.)

Since this mousse would take too long to jell, our instructor had made a similar one, earlier, for us to taste. Everyone looked expectant. A carafe of red wine was passed. We filled our glasses. The mousse appeared shivering on its plate. Gray, gelatinous, pimpled with black caviar; it looked like the sort of "thing" that tries to take over the world on a late Sci-Fi movie. But it tasted divine. We refilled our wine glasses. The mousse passed back and forth. Everyone began talking.

Meanwhile, the little assistant, a student from Hunter, was washing the utensils. ("Secret of French cooking," I wrote, "is having a little assistant to wash up as you cook.")

Bzzzzz! The oven timer went off – a few of us nearly dropped our wine glasses. Duck turning time. Our instructor took a big bulb baster and drew off several cups of grease, before she skillfully flipped both birds and lowered the oven to 350 degrees. We all raised our glasses and toasted her. The room had gotten noisy. It sounded like a cocktail party. Our instructor finally regained our attention by shouting: "Pommes de terre!" She held up a ripple-cutter and showed us how to thin-slice a raw, peeled potato, turning it each time so that the slices emerged cross-hatched, like tiny round waffles. "How darling!" everyone said. We passed the carafe. ("Buy ripple potato-cutter," I wrote, "to make darling French fries.") The rest of the potatoes were handed to the little assistant to finish. (I wrote: "Secret of French cooking is to have little assistant do boring work.")

I smiled happily. I was learning a lot of secrets. The carafe came my way. Why not? I poured myself another glassful. At the end of the bar, people were arguing about restaurants. "I was at Lutèce just last week," the woman in the ultra-suede dress told the IBM executive. "You can't beat Le Cirque," he insisted. "La Caravelle," someone stated defiantly.

Since I usually dine at Pizza Heaven, I kept quiet.

"Caramelizing the sauce," our instructor announced. We tried to focus on her as she put three tablespoons sugar and one-quarter cup red wine vinegar on to boil. The secret, she told us, is to swirl the pan until the contents are mahogany brown. The pan went round and round. So did my head. Now the very hot duck stock, which had been simmering, was strained of its vegetables, added to the caramelized sugar, and stirred with a wire whisk. ("Buy wire whisk.") Two tablespoons arrow root blended with one-third cup Madeira were whisked in and simmered. Finally, blanched orange-peel slivers (four oranges' worth) went in. Whisk, whisk.

The timer buzzed. Duck check. Their juices were running clear; our ducks were done. "Hooray!" We raised our glasses.

The vegetables in the roasting pan must be deglazed. (I wrote: "Remove fat, add one-half cup Madeira, and boil down to a few tablespoons.") As the vegetables deglazed, the class looked more and more glazed. Everyone was talking. It was just like a party: the guests carousing while the hostess, totally ignored, works frantically.

The glazed vegetables were strained out, and their juice was combined with the sauce, simmered for 10 minutes, before the final touch: three tablespoons of orange liqueur. *Fini.* The instructor seized her poultry shears to divide the ducks: up the breast bone, down the spine, and across into four sections. ("Buy poultry shears. Only sensible way to carve duck." My handwriting had begun to slant uphill.) The little assistant handed each of us a plate of duck and French fries. We all poured ourselves another glass of wine. The duck smelled divine – but seemed to be mostly bones. Disappointing for so much work. However, the rich, liquory sauce was sensational. ("Pour sauce in shot glass," I wrote. "Throw out duck.") We passed the sauce-boat.

A salad appeared from somewhere. We drank the last of the red wine. But then someone found a jug of rosé that belonged to another class. We passed the jug. Our instructor was racing through dessert now – which, for some reason, turned out to be a pineapple instead of pears. I was confused – but dessert went nicely with the rosé. Everyone sounded witty and charming. Such *fun* people! What a great evening!

"My God," the instructor whispered to her assistant. "They were supposed to leave at 8 – it's 9:20 now and they're still drinking." She quickly made coffee.

As we staggered out, we had to pass the shop. All the equipment that I needed seemed, mysteriously, to be for sale there. Outside on the steps I stopped, and swaying slightly, leaned against a wall to scribble my last comment: "Secret of French cooking is French wine."

Later, I covered the New York Harbor Patrol's Underwater Recovery Team – a great summer assignment despite the two bodies we pulled up: one from the Hudson River and the other from a Bronx reservoir.

THE SCUBA COPS

OFFICER NUTLEY FORGOT THE MUSTARD. They were in the middle of the Hudson River aboard a Harbor Patrol launch, making sandwiches: salami, Swiss, liverwurst on rye.

And no mustard! Sgt. Joe Mottle and Officer Bill Reddan of the Underwater Recovery Team had been giving him a hard time, threatening to toss him overboard so he could swim to the nearest deli. Whoever heard of Swiss on rye with no mustard?

The police launch was anchored in deep water just off 76th Street. Between the boat and shore an orange buoy with a red flag bobbed, indicating "Divers below." The scuba team had been down all morning, swimming two-man shifts, searching for evidence: a subway locker key thrown into the river by Croatian terrorists. A bomb found in that locker had exploded, killing a policeman. Periodic streams of air bubbles broke the river's surface; unseen below, divers Mark Walsh and Jim Mottle (Joe's brother) swam slowly back and forth, following a search pattern, gloved hands probing the mud. It was a tedious job. And the water is filthy there, between two huge Manhattan sewer outlets. Visibility near the bottom, even carrying underwater lights, was a poor six inches. Behind their bubbles clouds of silt rose, tracing black lanes through the river.

Above the polluted water it was a sunny day. Blue horizons, clean air. Apartment buildings on Riverside Drive thrust defined roofs at a bright sky. The launch rocked gently. Officer Nutley sliced some cheese. At that moment a motor dinghy pulled alongside. Diver Tom Power had been ashore picking me up, on assignment to write about the scuba team. Nutley's eyes lit up as he hurried on deck to give us a hand. "Welcome aboard," he called. "You wouldn't by any chance have any mustard on you?"

"Imagine the biggest junkyard in the world – you're crawling through it with your eyes closed – and it's underwater." Joe Mottle passed the pickles. "That's New York Harbor. You'll find anything below water you can find above. As long as people have access they're going to throw things in – fall in, jump in, dive in, drive in, capsize, drown. New York City has 576 miles of shoreline. And that's not including lakes and reservoirs. There's always something."

We were in the launch cabin eating sandwiches. Tom Power had gone back out with the small boat to bring in the divers, who were low on tank air.

"The Underwater Recovery Team is a unit of the New York Harbor Patrol," Sgt. Mottle told me. "That's the Harbor Police, mainly men like Officer Nutley here, who pilot boats that patrol city waters. Sort of an aquatic beat. Our work, on the other hand, is *under* the water. We're a small unit, six officers and a sergeant – all trained scuba divers. Most of our jobs fall into three categories: bringing up dead human bodies; recovering guns or other weapons used to commit crimes; locating submerged cars (stolen cars, cars used in crimes, cars with victims inside). Last year we completed 300 assignments with a 90% recovery rate.

"You can be down looking for a gun and bump into a body," Bill Reddan added, "or vice versa. We're never sure what we'll find. Visibility in the rivers is seldom more than a few inches, so you learn to tell by feel whether you've found a gun or a piece of pipe, a mattress or a body."

"Meanwhile, you're being tossed about, swept along by currents," Joe Mottle said. "The worst currents are in the East River; Hell Gate earns its name. The Hudson, south of George Washington Bridge, is tidal with a mud bottom and silt buildup. The East River has a deep rock-and-gravel bed full of enormous boulders. It's easier to locate objects on a hard bottom, but a diver can get ripped on those rocks if he isn't careful. Under the Brooklyn Bridge there's 70 feet of water with currents so strong a gun will travel a hundred feet before it reaches bottom. You have to calculate which direction the current was moving when it went in and how far it may have traveled. On the channel side of the bridge, we've seen a sunken railway barrage still full of old wooden boxcars. Hundreds of years of junk. Jim and Benny found a 200-year-old anchor last summer and the team presented it to South Street Seaport for the Bicentennial."

Outside on deck, Mark and Jim were getting out of their wetsuits. Unfastening weight belts, pulling off gloves and molded rubber hoods, peeling away their skin-tight rubber jackets. Flippers, masks, and steel tanks leaned against the gunwales, dripping muddy pools.

"What have we got to eat?" Jimmie appeared in the cabin door stripped down to black wet-suit tights, followed by Mark. Tall, well-built cops. When they saw me, both started forward to shake hands, then hesitated. "Better not," Jimmie explained politely. "We probably stink."

Joe handed them thick cheese sandwiches. "Our reporter wants to know what you guys found down there today."

Mark shook his mop of wet hair. "Nothing – the usual junk: beer cans, baseballs, hub caps, rusted fenders, bicycles, shopping carts, an old refrigerator... "

Officer Nutley turned around, "Did you happen to look inside to see if there was any mustard?"

THE CASE OF THE MAN UNDER THE PIER

"Most of our jobs are bodies." 9 a.m. Monday. Below an abandoned Hudson River pier off Bank Street in Greenwich Village. Bright innocent sunlight. Rotting wood. A gaping hole.

Jim Mottle hoisted a 40-pound air tank and strapped it on Tom Power's back. Big Benny Manuella was already lowering himself over the side of the police boat. He grinned up at us from the water, frog-eyed through his plastic mask, sucked in on his mouthpiece, and sank, oily river closing over his head. Out of sight, Tom watched him disappear.

"Why aren't they diving together?" I asked.

"Too dangerous." Jim pointed to the close rows of rotted piling. "There isn't room under there for two divers. Look at the thing. Suppose it collapses? We'll only lose one man. Tommy's ready to go down in case Benny needs help."

We stared into the oil soup below; debris slapped the sides of the boat. On the dock an ambulance waited. Blue uniformed precinct cops milled about watching us.

"When did it happen?"

"Saturday night, late," Jim said. "Nobody's supposed to be on that pier – you can see it's fenced off – but it was a warm night and people were there. Whoever it was fell through the hole. They heard splashing two or three minutes, then nothing."

"Nobody dropped him a belt or a shirt sleeve?"

"I don't know. Somebody did report it to the precinct. They tried grappling yesterday, but it was obstructed."

We watched Benny's air bubbles float up past the rotted pilings.

"See there," Tom pointed. "A blue claw crab. You can tell there's a sewer outlet nearby. Blue claws love sewers. Eels too. In winter, you know when you're coming near an outlet because the water gets warmer. And then you see the Charmin floating by like snow. Man, that stuff can really clog your regulator: 'gloop.' No air. And you come up fast, festooned like a Christmas tree."

"Movie film is worse," Jim said. "And IBM tape. There's miles of movie film rolling around in New York waters. Transparent, you can't see it. And it's not biodegradable; it's forever. Wraps around you – like swimming into an octopus. Your partner has to cut you loose."

"I got him; down here." Benny shouted to us from under the pier, 15 feet out.

"Need any help?" Tom yelled back. Benny shook his head and submerged again. "A body weighs a lot waterlogged," Tom explained. "Before decomposition sets in and gases start to form. In summer bodies decompose fast, swelling up with gases that raise them to the surface in three or four days. But if they go down in winter, they stay down until spring. The first warm weather and bodies start popping up all over the harbor – 'floaters' we call them – and the Harbor Patrol is busy picking them up.

"Not very pretty. It's nobody's favorite job going down for a body." Tom shook his head. "But we find them faster – they haven't begun to decompose – and so they look better. It's easier on the family who have to identify them. Less grief. Grappling's a slow hit-or-miss operation and the hooks can mess up flesh. If a body's caught it may never come up. Unless we go down for it."

Movement in the water below. A bare human back broke the surface, head hanging down trailing wet black hair, flesh bleached gray. As it rose higher in the water, we could see Benny's shoulder. Tom reached over and grabbed the torso while Benny swam out from under. Together they floated the body – a white man, shirtless, wearing dark pants, socks, and shoes – while Jim slipped ropes underneath to lift him. The precinct cops were standing on the seawall now, waiting. As the body jerked up out of the water, it rolled sideways – absolutely stiff – bent arms sticking out chest high, fingers open and clutching in a pitiful supplicating gesture. Blood was pouring from the nose and open mouth. I choked.

"It's all right," Jimmie said quickly. "They always bleed when they surface, pressure or something; it's normal."

The body rested on the boat prow. A thin, long-haired man in his 40s, eyes shut, bloody gashes across his forehead and beaky nose, ears very purple. As the divers maneuvered the boat closer to the seawall, I stared at the gray, reaching arms; they wavered in the air when the boat rocked.

"Is that rigor mortis?"

Jimmie nodded. "The arms are always in that position – muscles tighten – you find them lying on the bottom just like that."

Two precinct cops leaned over, grabbing the ropes, and hoisted the body, arms waving stiffly, onto the seawall. I watched as they examined it, slitting open the trousers with a knife, searching for identification. Nobody knew who he was.

The divers climbed ashore. Their blue and white van was parked nearby with Mark at the wheel. Benny went inside to change while Jim stood beside the precinct sergeant filling out a report.

I watched the cops remove a wet pack of cigarettes from the slit pockets and a black coin purse: small change, mostly pennies. They examined the head wounds: foul play? The medical examiner would decide. Nobody missed him, I thought. No keys – no apartment. Skinny, malnourished, he must have been a vagrant. Maybe from the Bowery? So perhaps he was drunk when he fell through. I hoped so. Too drunk to have understood his ugly, frightening death...

Tom Power took my arm and led me away. "It's nobody's favorite job," he said gently.

Maybe the jokes make it bearable: the jokes and camaraderie. But I wasn't laughing anymore. As we zipped along the Belt Parkway in the blue and white van, they tried to cheer me up. We were going to a relatively easy assignment now, the Rockaway Coast Guard Station to replace a damaged propeller on a launch. The team does underwater repair work for the Coast Guard as well as for the Police Harbor Patrol.

"Some of our jobs do have happy endings," Jim told me. "Did you see the movie 'Poseidon Adventure'? Well about 18 months ago, the team had its own 'Poseidon Adventure.' A tugboat that had been pushing a barge off Rockaway hit an obstruction and flipped over upside down. We got the call to stand by in our gear – a helicopter was on its way to pick up the divers."

"See, when a boat turns upside down fast," Tom explained, "pockets of air get caught in the hull – and as long as that air lasts there's a possibility that some crew trapped inside might still be alive. Benny, Charlie O'Donnell, and a former team member, Bob Byrne, were on duty that day. Everybody's supposed to be qualified to jump out of a chopper. Some of us are former Navy divers, trained in air/sea rescue:

dropping 30 feet into the ocean. But we don't get much practice.

"Anyhow, those guys didn't have time to worry about that. They barely had time to fix up a couple of extra tanks. And the next thing they know they're looking down from the 'copter. They can see the tug floating hull up and Coast Guard boats waiting to pick up survivors. Then they're splashing into the Atlantic, hanging onto their tanks. Fortunately, underwater visibility's better in the ocean than the rivers. They locate the hatch and swim up the ladder. Inside it's pretty dark – they begin using underwater flashlights – swimming through rooms, banging into floating furniture, looking for bodies, trying to find their way up into the hull.

"Finally they heard tapping, and they surface in the air space. There are these three crewmen scared stiff, standing on the machinery to keep their heads above water. And one of them is trying to commit suicide. He knows he can't swim, and he's trying to swallow water. So Charlie and Byrne take the other two guys, explaining how they're going to go back down underwater through the tug and swim out. But this one guy is still trying to commit suicide. Well Benny here's strong as a horse... "

Benny smiled modestly.

"So Benny doesn't argue. He grabs this guy, shoves an airpiece in his mouth, and carries him struggling – by brute force – swimming for both of them. All of those crewmen survived. But this one guy just couldn't believe it. You never saw anybody so grateful. He couldn't stop shaking Benny's hand.

The van turned into the Coast Guard Station. "Benny never talks about being a hero," Jim said. "What he likes to talk about is how he pulled Diana Nyad out of the East River when she got caught by currents on her first swim around Manhattan."

Benny Manuella grinned. "The guys are jealous. She was a real nice-looking girl, even all covered with grease."

THE CASE OF THE GUNS IN THE RIVER

The 138th Street Bridge connects Harlem to the South Bronx, and it seems to be a favorite place for criminals of both communities to dispose of their weapons. Two years ago, while searching for a .38-caliber revolver used in the shooting of a policeman, the team brought up not one, but two .38s along with 20 other handguns. Neither .38 proved to be the guilty weapon, but ballistic tests on the other guns proved that most had been involved in crimes.

Today for a change, the scuba cops had an exact location: a suspect had confessed dropping a murder weapon off the Harlem side of the bridge. Another .38. Currents are strong at this point in the Harlem River. Joe Mottle and Mark Walsh were in the motorboat under the bridge, sinking grapnels anchored to ropes, laying a search pattern. Not only would the divers have poor visibility, but they would also need to hang onto these ropes as they groped along the bottom to keep from being swept downriver.

"My mouthpiece is beginning to taste like an oilcan." Jim Mottle sat on boulders near the Harlem shore, adjusting his mask. The water around his flippers was rainbowed with oil slicks: ugly colors that scattered as he and Tom Power lowered themselves off the rocks, letting a 10 mph current sweep them along its surface until they caught hold of the buoy where Joe had anchored their ropes. As they followed the ropes downward, their underwater lights could be seen descending for several feet – then nothing.

Joe and I watched from the police launch. "Nobody really knows the long-term effects of pollution like this on a diver," he told me. "The team's only been in existence nine years. It was originally started on an experimental basis by two cops who were also sports divers, and who provided their own equipment. They were so successful – making recoveries in about one-fifth the time of other methods (grappling, magnets, hard-suit commercial divers) – that the department decided to form a unit. Everyone who joins does so voluntarily and has had experience as a diver. The force has neither money nor facilities to train divers.

"About one diver in 30 is able to pass our requirements, both physical and mental. You need strong nerves. I've seen good sports divers panic in a New York river; they can't see and they get caught on junk at the bottom. We've had divers swim blind into phone booths, old safes, and one time under the George Washington Bridge, a circus cage! That guy couldn't figure out what had him; every way he tried to swim – bars.

"The men get regular physical checkups and shots; they also attend fitness sessions at the Police Academy. We range in age from 28 to 36, and all of us, except the two youngest, Mark and Jimmie, are married and have families. The men get a lot of respiratory infections, skin rashes: we've had mono and hepatitis. But our safety record is good – only one diver, a founding member, left because of physical disability. He lost a finger.

"We've had some close calls though. Once Jim and Tom were looking for a helicopter that went down off the 23rd Street Marina – it's 50 to 60 feet deep there with big car-sized boulders. Tom is sweeping by with the current when he looks up; there's Jimmie hanging off a propeller, flapping like a sheet in the breeze. Tom freed him.

"You can see why we always dive in pairs and need at least one man on the surface to keep the area clear. Those wet-suits we wear are really more for protection than warmth. When you see some of the slits in your rubber suit – and think how your flesh could have been laid open… " Sgt. Mottle shuddered.

"Tin, glass, and wire really cut up suits; if you ever fall in the river keep your shoes on. Our winter suits are for warmth. We also wear long johns under the suits to keep from freezing. We dive year 'round, even under ice. When Prospect Park Lake freezes, the team teaches a course in ice rescue for other cops – playing victims themselves so patrolmen can learn to assist without endangering their own lives."

Mark waved to us from the small boat; the divers were coming up. They had two guns.

"Visibility was good today," Jim said cheerfully. "Almost a foot. You know, I think there are more guns in that river than fish." We examined the guns, a rusty snub-nosed .38 and a plastic toy.

"The toy was probably used in a stickup," Joe said. "Why else toss it in the river?" But we'll send this one to ballistics." He placed the .38 in a plastic bag to prevent more rusting as it dried.

Tom Power entered the cabin with a towel around his neck, eating a peanut butter and jelly sandwich. "Irish pastry," he explained, giving us a bite. "Helps you stay down."

THE CASE OF THE CAR OFF THE FERRY

Brown Dog was barking something fierce. "Probably a gull landed on our pier," the divers told me. We were loading the launch at the team's base, a dilapidated sanitation pier off 52nd Street, Brooklyn, which they share with the Fire Department and the Harbor Patrol. Brown Dog, a big cheerful mongrel, is the base mascot. "She simply showed up one day to defend us from seagulls," Charlie O'Donnell said.

This morning the team was going out to locate a submerged car in Newtown Creek. A routine stolen car job – "except that everybody hates Newtown Creek," Bill Reddan explained. "Like doing time in hell. It's dead water off the East River; no visibility and a high acid content. You can feel the water get thicker as you go down – like diving in syrup.

"When bubbles break the surface off Newtown Creek, it isn't fish, it's chemical oxidation from waste on the bottom. Every little scratch you didn't know you had begins to fester."

As the launch headed out into the Upper Bay, leaving a sharp cold wake behind, I asked the divers what they expected to find.

"Locating a submerged car's mostly routine checking," Bill answered. "Unless we discover a body inside. You'd be surprised the number of people who commit suicide by driving their cars into the water."

Off to our left, the Staten Island ferry passed. Charlie O'Donnell pointed. "One of the strangest car jobs we ever had was off that ferry. Benny, Jimmie, and I were on duty."

Jim Mottle nodded. "There were hundreds of passengers aboard that day, but no one could tell us for sure what had happened. It seems the ferry had just begun loading cars for the Manhattan trip. One of the men securing them happened to turn around. He thought there'd been a car there. Only there wasn't. Then everybody started shouting: passengers on the upper decks, passengers in other cars. They'd all just seen an automobile shoot through the air – maybe a hundred feet – land in the water and disappear. It was so spectacular that most people believed they were witnessing some sort of stunt. Maybe a movie being filmed.

"And nobody could be sure they'd seen anyone inside the car – it had been too quick. Water off the ferry slip is 60 feet deep; it took us a while to find that car. We couldn't believe it had traveled so far. Finally we located it using underwater lights. Benny swam up to look in the windshield – and nearly jumped out of his suit. There was a woman looking straight back at him, just sitting there, both hands still on the steering wheel! Inside the car, we discovered a young man hunched over on the seat beside her, strapped in by a seat belt. We brought them both up. But what they were doing down there was a complete mystery."

"Later we found out that the woman was a Staten Island doctor's wife," Charlie said. "And the young man turned out to have been her son – a spastic. The only thing we could figure is that he may have had a sudden seizure and struck the gas pedal."

The boat slowed, approaching Newtown Creek.

"She was just sitting there?" I asked. "Then how did she look?"

Charlie rubbed his mustache. "Surprised," he said. "She looked surprised."

HOW I BECAME SOLVENT

IT WAS AN ORDINARY WINTER ASSIGNMENT that determined my future. My editor at the *New York Sunday News* magazine needed something to cheer readers during an extended "snowed-in" season. I was sent out to discover it. "Shaking Off the Blues," I wrote, "Belly Dancing, Bag-piping, Juggling, and Other Healthful Diversions." I even attended a plunge in the ocean off Coney Island with the Iceberg Athletic Club. This quickly written piece appeared the following Sunday, illustrated by a full-page photo of a voluptuous belly dancer (to make it appear longer). The next week, while recovering from a cold, I got a phone call from a recruitment firm asking me to interview for a speechwriting job at a Fortune 500 company in New Jersey. The CEO who hired them had been told that his speeches were dull and humorless. He had not liked any of their applicants. "Why can't you find me a writer like this?" he asked them, holding up my *News* story. Had he gone mad? What they saw was the dancer! Once this contretemps had been straightened out, the head recruiter called the *News* for my phone number.

Oddly, my "real" writing life ended there, although I grew skilled and more valuable to the world that began to pay my wages. Corporate writing is hard and I rarely saw the sun. However, I am not on the streets and can pay to print this collection. The earliest pieces are not complete stories, but memories, unexpected flashes, stirred by some image that cuts through the murk of childhood. Many are set in summer; hot Ohio summers of swimming, porches, bare feet, cut grass…

Now in these hot New York City rooms, where I grow relentlessly older, summer is hellish. Sweating. Blinds drawn. Heat pressing against the window glass. Yet I can still feel the sun on my wet shoulders and the rough mat of the board that throws me high into the air – somersaulting into a rush of cold blue water.

I am finally that wondrous thing, older – but wiser. Will the Library of Congress think so?